WorKsHop
Essentials

Planning and Presenting
Dynamic Workshops

Paula Jorde Bloom

NEW HORIZONS
EDUCATIONAL CONSULTANTS AND LEARNING RESOURCES

LAKE FOREST, ILLINOIS 60045-0863

Design – Stan Burkat
Illustrations – Marc Bermann

New Horizons
Educational Consultants and Learning Resources
P.O. Box 863
Lake Forest, Illinois 60045-0863
(847) 295-8131
(847) 295-2968 FAX

Library of Congress Cataloging-in-Publication Data

Bloom, Paula J.
        Workshop essentials: planning and presenting
    dynamic workshops / Paula Jorde Bloom. - 1st ed.
        p. cm.
        Includes bibliographical references and index.
        LCCN: 00-103512
        ISBN: 0-9621894-4-8

        1. Workshops (Adult education) 2. Training.
    3. Interpersonal communication. I. Title

    LC44.2.J67 2000   374.973
                                       QBI00-499

Printed in the United States of America

Acknowledgements

This book represents the collective wisdom I have garnered through the years as a workshop presenter and attendee. The ideas have been field-tested in church basements, hotel ballrooms, and college classrooms with thousands of early childhood teachers and administrators. The feedback these participants have given me has been an invaluable source of personal enrichment as I've worked to perfect my own presentation skills.

For a person like me who is fastidious about documenting original sources in the academic writing I do, writing this book was quite a challenge. Tracking down original sources for training tips and techniques is a bit like unraveling a spider web. Some of the terrific ideas included on the following pages were taken from notes I had scrawled on the back of conference programs. Others were shared with me (often in a hallway or parking lot) by participants in my workshops. Wherever possible, I have cited sources. I apologize if I have inadvertently omitted any.

I am indebted to my colleagues at the Center for Early Childhood Leadership for helping me understand how diverse good training can look. They are an amazing collection of trainers in their own right, each with a unique and special style.

I am grateful to Bernadette Herman, Donna Rafanello, Eileen Eisenberg, Tim Walker, Jill Bella, and Catherine Cauman for their careful editing of the manuscript. Their thoughtful critiques of my writing are deeply appreciated. Thanks also to Sara Starbuck, Rachel Meyer, and Heather Knapp for their assistance in tracking down resources.

Finally, I am forever thankful to my husband Darrell for his support, patience, and encouragement. He is the perfect partner, in living and in learning.

About the Author

Paula Jorde Bloom holds a joint appointment as director of the Center for Early Childhood Leadership and professor of early childhood education at National-Louis University in Wheeling, Illinois. She received her master's and doctoral degrees from Stanford University. Known for her fast-paced and energizing presentation style, Paula is a frequent keynote speaker and workshop presenter at state, national, and international conferences. Dr. Bloom is also the author of several other widely read books, including *Living and Learning with Children*, *Avoiding Burnout*, *A Great Place to Work*, *Blueprint for Action*, and *Circle of Influence*.

Contents

Introduction

Like you, I have attended dozens of workshops during my career. Sometimes I've walked away feeling energized. I've gleaned new insights and in some small way been transformed by the experience. Other times, though, I've left feeling bruised and disappointed. I've resented my time being wasted and an opportunity for learning lost. However, in both kinds of workshops, I've learned a great deal about workshop presentation — the essential ingredients that make an engaging and memorable learning experience and the ingredients that make learning tedious, boring, and difficult to understand.

There is a myth that good workshop leaders are born, not made; that they are somehow endowed with an innate ability to inspire and transform. I don't believe that. Like playing the piano or whipping up a great soufflé, conducting a dynamic, high-impact workshop takes practice. It is a skill that can be learned and continually refined. An inspiring workshop may look effortless, but that smooth, crafted performance by the workshop leader comes about only through careful planning and preparation.

In my experience, many workshop leaders have content expertise but lack training in instructional design, adult learning, and group facilitation. Such leaders may have been asked to give workshops because they have advanced degrees or many years of experience, not because they have the repertoire of skills needed to plan and implement successful professional development experiences. They end up conducting workshops that fail to inspire and motivate participants to make the changes in attitudes, knowledge, and behavior needed to improve job performance.

Because early childhood is a field with limited resources, we can't afford to waste time or squander dollars on poorly planned training. Hit-or-miss approaches to professional development take a toll on our workforce, failing to spark and sustain the enthusiasm needed for lifelong learning. There is simply no way we can achieve our goal of providing high-quality services for children and families if we can't build and maintain a competent and capable workforce.

I hope this book provides the tools needed to plan and implement professional development workshops that ignite a passion for learning. If you are new to the role of presenting, this book can help you master the basics of workshop design, organization, delivery, and dealing with anxiety. If you are a seasoned trainer, you'll find dozens of tips and techniques that you can use to liven up your workshops to make them even more effective.

What Is a Workshop?

Because the requisite qualifications for working in early childhood education are so minimal, in-service training in the form of workshops has become a prime vehicle for instilling good teaching and management practices. A workshop is different from a formal lecture, a keynote speech, or a sharing session at a staff meeting. While all these educational experiences may have information dissemination as their goal, a workshop is a unique type of professional development experience that is designed to actively engage participants in the learning process. Workshops motivate participants by making connections between the content and their life experiences, striving for personal relevance of ideas.

The purposes of workshops are as varied as their catchy titles. They may be sponsored by organizations for their employees alone or offered as part of a smorgasbord of learning opportunities at a local, state, or national conference. The goal may be to help participants understand popular child development or management theories, learn new teaching or supervisory strategies, or address ethical dilemmas and other professional issues.

Anticipated outcomes of workshops also differ. Some work to change participants' attitudes on important issues, others to increase participants' knowledge base about early childhood concepts; still others attempt to instill new behaviors in the participants when they return to their jobs.

Time frames for workshops may vary from one hour to several days. The time frame, anticipated outcomes, and overall goals of the workshop impact the design and delivery of the content. This volume will help you maximize the time you have with participants to achieve your desired outcomes.

Three Hats of a Workshop Leader

In these pages I use the terms *trainer*, *presenter*, and *facilitator* interchangeably. There is a subtle distinction between these workshop roles, but in the course of even an hour-long workshop, effective workshop leaders wear each of these hats.

Trainers

Trainers see themselves as catalysts for learning. They establish desired outcomes before the workshop and then implement a plan of action to achieve those outcomes with participants during the session. The outcomes may focus on specific skills or knowledge that relate to effective teaching or administrative performance. Active involvement by participants is key to their internalizing important concepts. The visual aids trainers use reinforce learning points. The questions trainers ask evaluate learning. Like the coach of a star athlete, a trainer uses techniques such as observation, questioning, explaining, and modeling to help scaffold a trainee's level of skill or awareness to the next level of competence.

Presenters

Presenters inform, motivate, entertain, describe, and advocate for a particular course of action. Presenting is largely one-way communication. In most instances the presenter is presumed to be an expert whose role is to transmit information to the audience. The visual aids presenters use are intended to communicate data or information that support their message. Unlike trainers, presenters usually answer questions rather than ask them.

Facilitators

Facilitators don't try to convert or inform. Their role is primarily to ask questions and skillfully elicit from the group different points of view. Rather than having predetermined outcomes like the trainer, or perceiving oneself as the expert like the presenter, the facilitator's outcomes emerge as the group processes information about a particular problem or issue. Their visual aids such as the flip chart, are intended to record ideas, not to inform or change behavior.

In wearing the hats of trainer, presenter, and facilitator, workshop leaders need both didactic modes of delivery for passing information on to the participants and evocative modes to draw information and meaning from participants. The leader's goal in all these roles, however, is to model respectful listening, the honoring of various perspectives, sharing, trusting, and risk-taking — behaviors that he or she hopes participants will take back to their organizations.

Effective Workshop Leaders — Some Commonalities

If you've attended a number of engaging and memorable workshops, you know that effective workshop leaders come in all shapes and sizes. Some are outgoing and charismatic, while others are decidedly more low-key and reflective in their approach. Presentation style should be like your thumbprint — unique to you. It is your special personality blended with the technical skill you have crafted over the years.

There is no one best style. There are characteristics, however, that effective workshop leaders seem to share. The four that I think are most important are their passion about their subject, their flexibility in their approach, their reflection about their performance, and their willingness to take risks to try new instructional strategies and techniques.

Passion

Passion about the subject is essential for credibility. You simply can't ignite excitement in the hearts and minds of your workshop participants if you aren't excited about your topic. Effective workshop leaders know that their enthusiasm about the topic is communicated to participants verbally and nonverbally in what they say and what they do. Passion also regulates commitment. If you don't feel passionate about the subject, you won't have the desire to prepare fully for your presentation. And if you are not prepared, you can't communicate the subject matter with poise and confidence. If you give a presentation on a topic that you are not sincerely committed to, you may come across as disingenuous and a fraud. You simply can't fake passion.

Flexibility

Flexibility in meeting the needs of the group and the situation at hand is essential if you are going to make your workshop a meaningful experience for all participants. Early childhood educators tend by nature to be flexible in their professional lives. We pride ourselves on "going with the flow" in adapting our work to meet the unexpected demands of children and their families. This same flexibility is also essential in working with adults.

While it is important to have a workshop agenda, a willingness to modify that agenda is crucial if you are going to be responsive to the idiosyncratic needs of each group of workshop participants. While you will experience certain commonalities among all groups you train in a particular topic, each group has its unique needs and interests. The difference between a good presentation and an outstanding presentation is often in those subtle midcourse adjustments that presenters make to accommodate the special needs of the group.

Being flexible as a trainer also means being ready to accommodate any and all exigencies that arise in the workshop setting. I arrived at one workshop to find that the building janitor had the only key to the storage room where the overhead projector and flip charts were kept. The janitor, of course, was away on vacation. On another occasion the caterer didn't show up with the boxed lunches, and we had to take a quick fieldtrip to a nearby deli for lunch.

One of my favorite examples of the primacy of Murphy's Law was the scorching hot summer day I was doing training in San Antonio when the air conditioning unit in the building stopped functioning. We ended up having to relocate the workshop to the basement of the building where it was a comparatively cool 85°. Unexpected events such as these can spell disaster if you are not willing to quickly adjust your plan to accommodate the situation. That means anticipating the unexpected and having a variety of contingency plans in your back pocket in case you need them.

Reflection

Reflection on practice is something that all effective workshop leaders engage in. They see themselves as lifelong learners regularly reflecting on their own growth. Even the pros, those individuals whom you would think had mastered all the tricks of the trade, engage in a kind of instant replay after each workshop they give. In this personal debriefing they ask themselves, What went well? What didn't go well? What could be done differently next time? They seek out candid feedback from participants and other trainers on ways that they can improve their craft. In short, they never stop improving.

Risk Taking

Risk taking, that disposition to venture into unknown territory to try new and different strategies, is essential for continued growth. The most effective workshop leaders I have watched in action are willing to be vulnerable, risk looking silly, and even flop when trying out a new strategy. They are bold and adventurous. They take their craft seriously, but they don't take themselves seriously. That means they are willing to go out on a limb and be a bit daring. It takes nerve to try out a new role-playing strategy, introduce a new prop, use a finger puppet, or sing the directions to a group activity instead of reciting them in the same monotone you've used before. Expanding your repertoire of instructional techniques will keep you revitalized as a trainer, stretching and growing, alert and rejuvenated.

Becoming a Skilled Workshop Leader is a Developmental Process

When I say that effective workshop leaders are made, not born, I certainly don't want to imply that the process happens overnight. To the contrary. If you talk to any of the pros in the field, they will tell you the process takes years. The progress from novice to expert involves both cognitive changes in the way they view their role as well as technical changes in the actual mastery of workshop presentation skills.

While I've never conducted any empirical research on the topic, my own experience and the personal stories of dozens of other presenters lead me to believe that the development journey of workshop leaders can be characterized by three stages. For lack of any clever names, I'll simply call them Stages 1, 2, and 3.

Stage 1: Where is my script?

Those new to the role, Stage 1 presenters, often try to model their presentation style after a successful presenter they have watched in action. They are self-conscious, overly anxious, and tend to magnify their own

presentation flaws. Presenters in this stage have a limited repertoire of instructional strategies and stick closely to those few they feel most comfortable with. They have prepared "packaged" workshops, a kind of dog-and-pony show where the same workshop script is played regardless of the needs of different audiences.

Stage 1 presenters tend to be egocentric in their perspective, focusing on the content and information they want to impart rather than the learning needs of the participants. They are preoccupied with what they want to say and what participants need to know. Consequently they can be rigid, preferring to stick to their script rather than adapting to the needs of the group. Most of all, they want to be liked. They read evaluations for confirmation that they did a good job rather than for insights about how they could improve.

Stage 2: What are the needs of the participants?

Presenters who have found their own voice and style have reached Stage 2. They have learned to trust their intuition and instincts and are more flexible and genuine in their presentation style. They feel more comfortable in front of an audience and are beginning to expand their repertoire of instructional strategies. They do less *talking at* participants and are beginning to ask more open-ended questions.

The most significant change that takes place between Stage 1 and Stage 2 is the shift in orientation from teaching to learning, from teacher-centered to learner-focused. Stage 2 presenters are more comfortable with training strategies based on discovery, participation, and involvement. They are beginning to ask, "How can I facilitate this group's learning?" rather than, "How can I get my point across?" They are less concerned with being liked and more focused on how they can achieve desired learning outcomes.

Stage 3: How can I adapt my style to capitalize on teachable moments?

Stage 3 presenters have achieved a comfortable rhythm in their presentation style. They are able to alter their plans and make subtle shifts in the content and delivery of their material as the situation demands. Stage 3 presenters have the capacity to monitor and control their thinking while they are thinking. They engage in a kind of metacognitive or "out-of-body" awareness of what they are doing while they are engaged in different tasks and activities. In other words, they are aware not only of what they are saying, but of just how they are saying it. They also have an overall awareness of everything happening in the environment while they are focusing on one thing.

Stage 3 presenters are very audience sensitive. Their goal is to empower the audience, to help participants become active agents in their own learning. Because they have a wide range of instructional strategies at their command, they can seize opportunities that arise and create teachable moments that are unplanned and unscripted. Stage 3 presenters relish feedback and see each workshop as a way to grow in their understanding of human behavior. They genuinely believe they learn as much from a workshop as the participants do.

If you are new to the role of workshop presenting, be patient with yourself. If you are still at Stage 1, wanting to be a clone of some dynamic, fire-and-brimstone orator you once watched in action, that is okay. Your developmental journey as a trainer has just begun. Cull the best of what you have witnessed and begin to meld it with your own unique strengths. Your style will emerge in time. If you are open to self-improvement, willing to modify and adapt, and see each workshop you give as a precious opportunity to refine your skill base, in time you will gain the poise and confidence that seem so effortless in Stage 3 presenters.

The Importance of Experiential Learning

This book is committed to the proposition that active, participatory, experiential learning is essential if you are to inspire lasting changes in attitudes, knowledge, and behavior in those who attend your workshops. Using the experiential approach, the leader provides numerous opportunities during the workshop for participants to share life experiences and learn from each other.

Experiential learning takes individuals beyond mere awareness of principles to actually applying new skills and techniques. Trainers grounded in an experiential approach intersperse content with activities in which participants can process new ideas and practice them. Trainers must be adept not only at introducing concepts clearly and supplying specific workplace examples, but also at asking pointed questions and providing feedback that helps participants clarify and internalize their new knowledge and skills.

The goal of experiential approaches is to help participants become active agents in their own learning. Instead of viewing people as passive recipients of new knowledge and expertise, trainers using an experiential learning approach deliberately draw on participants' past and present experiences to enrich the learning process. These experiences can illuminate theoretical concepts and bring greater understanding.

David Kolb defines experiential learning as the process whereby knowledge is created through the transformation of the experience of the learner who is at the center of the learning process. He believes our job as educators is not only to implant new ideas, but also to help participants dispose of or modify old ones. In many cases, resistance to new ideas stems from their conflicts with old beliefs that are incompatible with the new. If the training process includes opportunities for participants to examine and test current beliefs and theories, then receptivity to new ideas and a willingness to integrate them into their belief systems will be facilitated.

Theory is learned through action and interaction, through relating to one's own experience. Cognitive learning requires attention to affective learning.

Elizabeth Jones

Creating a Safe Environment for Learning

In your role as workshop leader, you are responsible for creating a safe, nonthreatening environment in which learning can take place. This means managing the content, process, and environment. The content of the workshop is the actual information you hope to communicate. The process includes the approaches and strategies you use to deliver the content. The environment includes the physical and psychological surroundings of the workshop session, including the location, room arrangement, and tone of the training.

Creating a climate of respect is essential to the success of any workshop. How adults are treated in your workshop affects their receptivity to learning. The tone you set as you greet participants, introduce the topic, and listen attentively to the examples they share has an impact on the workshop outcomes.

In setting an optimum climate for learning, here are a few points this book will help you think about.

The physical environment

- ✔ Is the space comfortable and aesthetically pleasing?
- ✔ Is the space neither too crowded nor too spacious?
- ✔ Are personal needs addressed?

The psychological environment

- ✔ Do interactions exude a spirit of mutual respect?
- ✔ Do participants see themselves as partners in the teaching-learning experience?
- ✔ Do participants perceive their differences as enriching?
- ✔ Are interactions supportive and caring?
- ✔ Do people feel free to express themselves openly?

The social environment

- ✔ Do participants know one another's names?
- ✔ Is the tone of the workshop warm and friendly?
- ✔ Is the expectation for collaboration, not competition?
- ✔ Do participants perceive one another as valuable resources?
- ✔ Are people eager to share information with one another?

What You Can Expect from this Book

Workshop Essentials provides the professional tools and techniques you need to plan and deliver a dynamic workshop, one that actively involves the participants in the learning process. You'll learn how to see a presentation from the audience's point of view and evaluate your effectiveness during and after the event. You'll learn new training strategies — practical tips and techniques that you can put into practice immediately.

The suggestions in this book can help you make your workshops come alive. You'll learn methods you can incorporate to involve learners fully and actively in the learning process. After reading this volume, you'll be better able to diagnose participants' needs, design content that meets those needs, deliver your ideas with impact, and measure the results of your training. Most important, you'll find in the following pages that workshops can be fun — for both you and the participants.

Let's begin!

Before You Say "Yes"

So you've been asked to give a workshop to a group of early childhood teachers at a large social service agency in your community. Your ego got a boost when the agency contact mentioned that you were recommended by preschool teachers who had attended a workshop you presented at a statewide conference the previous year. The date is free on your calendar, the honorarium is more than you have ever been paid before as a presenter. You are ready to accept the invitation and start packing your felt-tip markers.

Before you say "Yes" there are some things you should consider as you negotiate the specifics of your workshop contract. How you work out these details may make the difference between feeling calm and collected on the day of your workshop or spinning out of control.

This is the time, as well, to learn as much as you can about the audience. What you learn about the workshop participants may make the difference between just a good presentation and a truly memorable one.

Finally, spend some time taking an inventory of your skills. A review of what you currently do as a presenter will provide some insight into how you can challenge yourself to grow professionally in this next event. This chapter helps you in all three of these areas.

Negotiating the Specifics of Your Workshop

When we get a call to present a workshop, we are so thrilled that someone out there actually wants to hire us to do training, we don't stop and think about the fit between our needs and values as a workshop leader and the needs and values of the sponsoring organization. In talking to dozens of fellow presenters, I've found that problems often surface in two areas: a difference in expectations about the scope and anticipated outcomes of the workshop, and confusion in the logistical details of the event.

Scope and anticipated outcomes

I recall vividly the telephone conversation I had a few months back with the CEO of a small child care chain who asked me to do some training with the directors of his 15 centers. He began the conversation by saying, "These directors are having a problem with turnover at their centers, and I'd like you to do a daylong workshop on how to attract and retain quality staff." He was willing to work around my schedule and offered an enticing training fee.

Years ago, when I was a less seasoned trainer, I probably would have accepted the invitation at this point in the conversation and moved the discussion to finding a mutually agreeable training date. Now, with a great deal more experience under my belt, I posed a series of questions to him: What topics did he expect me to cover in one day with his 15 directors?

WHAT'S NEGOTIABLE HERE...

"Recruiting and interviewing strategies, legal issues in personnel management, and oh, yes, supervision and teamwork," he replied. What outcomes did he expect from my training? "That staff turnover would decrease at these centers, of course." Had his directors requested training in this area? "No, but they sure need it," he replied. Had he planned any focused follow-up to my workshop? "No, hadn't thought about that," he said.

I seized the opportunity to help inform this well-meaning entrepreneur. His hope that I would provide a "quick fix" for the problems plaguing his centers in just one day of training were both unrealistic and unreasonable. I told him that I thought my coming in for one day and giving surface attention to the important topics he outlined would do more damage than good. I then explained that if he was serious in his commitment to support his directors in resolving the staff turnover issues at their centers, I would be happy to come in for a half-day group discussion with the directors. We would talk about their concerns and together plan a workshop training schedule over six months to cover some of the topics he and others suggested.

I told him that it would take a minimum of six to nine full days of training to adequately cover what these directors would need to address the turnover issues he wanted to resolve. I also added that I would agree to do this only if he and his chief financial officer participated in the training. We ended our conversation on an amiable note, but I was not surprised that I never heard back from him.

Such is the reality of the world of early care and education — critical issues to resolve and limited human and financial resources to resolve them. It is crucial that you find out about the organization, its values, its goals, its agenda for change. When negotiating a contract to provide training, three particularly important questions to ask are

- ✔ Who decided on the training topic?
- ✔ What are the outcomes the organization hopes to achieve from the workshop?
- ✔ Is there a problem that this training is trying to solve?

The bottom line in negotiating your contract is never promise more than you can deliver. If there isn't a match between your values and expectations and those of the event planner, then one or both of you is sure to be disappointed.

Before finalizing any contract, I like to get some background information on the organization. I often ask an open-ended question in the conversation, such as, "Tell me about your agency." I have found that the person who contacts me to check on my availability and negotiate a contract often has one set of perceptions about what is expected in the training. I try to arrange to talk with other people in the organization to determine the variety of perceptions about the goals of the workshop. This additional data enriches the information I have to tailor my training to their needs. In addition, I request copies of newsletters, organizational brochures, and mission statements to get a deeper understanding of the culture of the organization.

While it isn't always possible to turn a one-day training workshop into an organizational commitment for continued professional development, I ask my contact what follow-up support participants will receive to help ensure that necessary changes in attitudes, behavior, and knowledge take place. I try to find out what resources the organization has committed to help make sure the training sticks. I have been pleasantly surprised on more than one occasion that this simple question has stimulated a wonderful discussion about the need for follow-up and the importance of ensuring that this single training event supports the larger professional development goals of the agency.

Logistical details

It is so easy for miscommunication to arise regarding the logistical details of a workshop because presenters are often contacted well before the arrangements for the event have been finalized. The conference planner or your contact at an agency sponsoring a training event may have only limited information about the physical setup of rooms, the availability of audiovisual equipment, or even the precise number of participants who will attend the event.

These details are important to discuss, however, because many of the logistical parameters of the workshop will affect your planning and design of the training. For example, the number of participants attending your workshop will affect your decisions about the type of activities to include. The amount of space and the arrangement of tables in the room will surely impact your choice of grouping strategies and interactive exercises. Even knowing what will be said in the introduction of you as the presenter will influence what you want say in your opening remarks. Finding out as much as you can beforehand minimizes the possibility of surprises on the day of the event. Some questions to ask your contact:

- ✔ How many participants will be attending?
- ✔ Will you have access to the training room at least one hour prior to the workshop?
- ✔ Will there be any business to conduct before your presentation starts?
- ✔ Who will be doing the introduction?
- ✔ Will someone be available before the workshop to assist with final room setup?
- ✔ Will someone be available during the day to troubleshoot?
- ✔ What are the food arrangements for the day?
- ✔ How large is the room?
- ✔ Are there any restrictions about using pushpins or masking tape on the walls?
- ✔ Is there an elevator or ramp for easy access to the room?
- ✔ What are the time limitations for the workshop?
- ✔ Will someone be available to assist with audiovisual equipment?
- ✔ Whose responsibility is it to duplicate handouts?

Just a word about space. In your negotiations, be sure to specify the actual square footage you will need for your workshop. In my experience, conference planners (especially those who work for hotels) tend to think that many more people can fit into a room than is comfortable. This is particularly important if you are planning any interactive activities that require people to get up and move around.

It isn't always possible, but if you can, find out what other events will be happening at the workshop location during the time of your session. I've had a couple disastrous situations in my career. One was a workshop where a bachelor party was being held in the room adjacent to my training room. The men were enjoying a lingerie fashion show! The hoots and whistles echoed through the paper-thin walls. Needless to say, the participants in my session didn't appreciate their jolly good time or the smell of the cigar smoke that wafted through the air. In another situation my training room was located right next to the laundry facilities at a convention center. By the time I finished my three-hour presentation, I felt like I was the one who had been tumbling around in the dryer.

In a letter confirming your understanding of the arrangements to the hosting organization, you should again specify your needs with respect to audiovisual equipment, the physical arrangement of chairs and tables, and the placement of flip charts, screen, and projectors. I think it is also a good idea to include a drawing of the room setup you would like.

If you are traveling to the event, ask the following questions about travel arrangements.

- ✔ Who will purchase airline tickets?
- ✔ What is the distance between the airport and the hotel?
- ✔ How far is the hotel from the workshop venue?
- ✔ Will someone pick you up from the airport?
- ✔ Will someone help transport workshop materials?

In addition, be sure to get the home telephone number of your contact and the name of an emergency contact in the event an unexpected change occurs in your travel plans. Things do go wrong. I've had flights cancelled during a snowstorm. I've had luggage diverted to another corner of the globe. And I've arrived at my hotel the evening before my workshop only to find out the host organization forgot to make reservations and the hotel was overbooked.

Finally, be sure to ask about publicity for the event. Impressions about you and the training experience are formed before the workshop begins. The descriptive brochure or flyer that participants receive describing the event shapes their expectations. If possible, ask if you can preview the copy before it goes to press. I have learned this lesson the hard way. At least a dozen times over my career, I have arrived at a workshop to find my name misspelled in the program, someone else's picture is printed next to my workshop description, or there is some factual error or typo in my biography.

To prevent the possibility of misunderstanding, I suggest you develop your own set of contracting questions and a form you can use to keep track of different events. Often you will make arrangements for a speaking engagement several months to a year before the actual event. Having this background information stored in a file folder along with your telephone notes and copies of correspondence will help you refresh your memory about the specifics of the contract you negotiated. This reduces the possibility of a misunderstanding later. In Appendix A you will find a copy of the profile form I use.

Knowing Your Audience

Understanding the background and expectations of the participants attending your workshop may be the single most important factor contributing to a successful presentation. In your discussions with the agency contact or conference planner, find out if attendance at your workshop is required or voluntary. If it is mandatory, ask if the workshop is part of a required in-service training requirement or part of a larger organization professional development plan. What incentives have been offered to attendees? Are people being paid for the day, or is attendance an overtime obligation? Participants' interest and willingness to attend the training sets the initial tone for the event.

A workshop is most effective when it is based on participants' real learning needs. Take some time before the workshop to learn about people's general background characteristics. What is their level of education and experience? What are some of the issues they are dealing with in their teaching and administrative roles? Are there any sensitive issues you should know about? This information will help you customize your content.

Knowing your audience means having a good understanding of their level of knowledge about the topic. Have they previously had training on this topic? What are some of their concerns regarding the topic? This information allows you to make adaptations in the design and content of the material presented to reflect the group's needs. If possible, arrange to talk to several of the participants prior to the training. One strategy I use is to develop some case studies using participant's real-life experiences and anecdotes which I write up before to the training. Such personalized touches enrich the training experience for those attending.

Find out if the participants know one another. Will they be wearing name tags, and how do they prefer to be addressed? Ask your contact person what attendees will be doing immediately before and immediately after your session. This information will be useful as you plan and design the specifics of your workshop. For example, if people will be driving a long distance to get to the training site, you may need to adjust the content and instructional strategies of the first part of your session so that people can get refreshed and reenergized for the day ahead.

Ask your contact if any guests will attend the workshop. Might their presence influence the participants' level of involvement or willingness to speak out? Find out the names of the movers and shakers in the group — those individuals who may impact the group dynamic in positive or negative ways. Finally, be sure to ask if anyone attending is non-English speaking, sight or hearing impaired, or has any physical disabilities. With this information you can make adjustments to accommodate special needs.

When you have established a relationship with the sponsoring organization, see if you can conduct a needs assessment prior to training to elicit more detailed information from participants. This can be done formally or informally. I use questionnaires and surveys as well as telephone interviews to elicit background information about individual participants and their level of knowledge and understanding of the topic. The bits and pieces of personal information I get serve a dual purpose. They help me tailor the content of the training to their needs and structure some icebreaker activities that are more personal and meaningful to the group.

The other advantage of conducting a needs assessment is that often I can suggest to the sponsoring organization relevant readings or specific things that participants can work on before coming to a workshop. Such preworkshop assignments jumpstart the training because before coming to the session, participants have thought about some of the topics to be discussed.

If you are presenting a workshop as part of an educational conference, you probably won't have the opportunity to conduct a needs assessment prior to making your presentation. You can, however, include in your workshop description some thought-provoking questions that will get your attendees thinking about your session before they arrive at the conference. In the opening of your workshop, you can then link your content to these questions.

Taking Stock

Accepting a contract to present a workshop provides a rich opportunity for you to refine your presentation skills. Take a few minutes now to reflect on the workshops you have presented in the past. Ask yourself the questions in the Workshop Skills Inventory on the following page. Be honest in your responses. The purpose of this activity is to help you think about ways you can use workshops as opportunities for your personal and professional growth. If you have never presented a workshop, use this inventory as a template for planning your first event.

After you have rated all items, review the pattern of responses you indicated under each of the columns, *seldom*, *occasionally*, and *consistently*. Think of those items you indicated that you do consistently as your workshop presentation strengths. These are skills and behaviors to build on. Those items that you seldom or occasionally do will become areas to focus on as you read this book. These are the areas that will help you improve your effectiveness as a workshop leader and achieve the goals that both you and your sponsoring organization want as a result of your presentation.

Workshop Skills Inventory

Directions: Read through each item. Check (✔) the column with the heading that best describes your behavior.
Key: **S** = seldom, **O** = occasionally, **C** = consistently.

	S	O	C
Before the workshop...			
I am clear about my workshop goals and desired outcomes.			
I tailor my presentation to the unique needs of each audience.			
In planning, I write down key ideas first and then build around them.			
I have structured the body of my presentation in a logical sequence.			
I have a plan for making smooth transitions from one topic to the next.			
I have a plan for how and when to use visual aids.			
My visual aids are simple, easy to read, and eye-catching.			
I think about questions that might be asked and practice responses.			
I make sure the physical space supports my goal of interactive learning.			
I plan content that provides a balance of theory and application.			
I plan content to build on participants' previous knowledge and experiences.			
I plan ways for participants to share insights with one another.			
I consider how my content fits into the broader training needs of participants.			
I prepare a checklist to confirm that everything is ready for my workshop.			
I rehearse my presentation until I am comfortable with the material.			
I arrive early to check on the room setup, food, and other logistics.			
I test all audiovisual equipment prior to beginning my workshop.			
During the workshop...			
My introduction is attention getting and establishes rapport.			
I include an overview of my presentation in my introductory remarks.			
I am able to channel the anxiety I feel into useful enthusiasm.			
I talk about situations and incidents that the audience has experienced.			
I include a preview as well as a review of main ideas as my workshop unfolds			
I communicate my ideas with energy and enthusiasm.			
I use my notes as a reminder, not a crutch.			
I use stories and anecdotes to amplify key points.			
I emphasize how participants can apply the concepts I present.			
My gestures are natural and do not distract from what I am saying.			
My voice is clear, controlled, and communicates confidence.			
I maintain eye contact with participants.			
I think not only about what I am saying, but how I say it.			
I can be heard in the back of the room.			
I manage the group dynamics so no one person dominates the discussion.			
My visuals can be seen from the back of the room.			
I listen respectfully to the comments and opinions of participants.			
I pause when making the transition from one point to the next.			
I pace myself so I don't feel rushed at the end of the session.			
My conclusion provides a summary of the key points I covered.			
After the workshop...			
I seek feedback from participants about the workshop's effectiveness in meeting their learning needs.			
I seek feedback from the workshop organizers about my effectiveness in meeting their professional development goals.			
I reflect on the day, noting ways to improve the workshop next time.			

You've Got to Reach Them to Teach Them

A workshop trainer needs to be concerned not only with what people learn — the nitty-gritty of the workshop content — but also with how people learn — the multiple ways that individuals perceive, process, and organize information. If you've done any training at all, you already know that your participants vary widely in their preferences; some prefer to read information, some prefer to listen, others like to discuss. Some jump right in and actively engage in small group exercises, while others prefer to observe quietly from the sidelines. Some participants seem to grasp complex concepts quickly; others struggle to comprehend the basic ideas you are trying to communicate. Some people process information out loud by asking a lot of questions and engaging in lively discussions; others process information in more quiet and reflective ways.

The cornerstone of our work with children is the recognition and appreciation of individual differences. We pride ourselves on structuring learning environments that are developmentally appropriate and address the needs of individual children. The same principle applies when we work with adults: no two adults respond in the same way to any workshop you give. You can maximize the likelihood that participants will internalize important concepts and make desired changes in their attitudes, knowledge, and behavior if the learning experiences you plan are based on knowledge about the diverse ways that adults learn.

This seems like a very basic concept. It is surprising, though, how often it is ignored, particularly by those new to the world of workshop presentation. Novice trainers often begin with the faulty assumption that participants in their workshops learn in the same way they themselves do. If they perceive information primarily through listening, they may give a two-hour workshop without any handouts or visuals. The workshop may be a hit with a few folks in the room, but it is guaranteed to leave the majority of participants feeling frustrated.

Think of it this way. If you are reading this book with a pair of glasses perched on the bridge of your nose, you wouldn't naïvely assume that the rest of the world could see as clearly through your lenses as you do.

Every person is like every person in some ways,
Every person is like some other person in some ways,
Every person is like no other person in some ways.

C. Kluckhohn &
H. Murray

So it is with adult learning. If trainers are to really connect and establish rapport with their audience, they must honor the different lenses through which people view the world. They must embrace the adage, "Different strokes for different folks."

This chapter provides a context for adult learning and explores some of the issues related to learning styles. It is not by any means intended to be exhaustive. I hope, however, that it will prompt you to think about the ways you can stretch your own instructional style to accommodate the diverse learners in your workshops.

We begin with a discussion about the characteristics of adult learners, some things that most adults have in common. From there, we look at learning styles, multiple intelligences, the importance of teaching to the whole brain, and how to engage the heart. The chapter concludes with a brief description of four types of learners you will typically find in your workshops.

Characteristics of Adult Learners

Adult learners share certain characteristics, and under the right circumstances they can be self-directed, self-motivated managers of their personal learning. If you design your workshop and implement instructional strategies that support the principles of adult learning, you'll increase the likelihood that the participants in your workshop will be committed to individual and group goals. Some things to keep in mind:

- **Adults bring a wide range of personal and professional experiences to each new learning situation.** The experiences adults have had impact what and how they learn. If you are to be successful as a workshop presenter, your instructional strategies need to validate and honor these varied experiences. You can do this by providing ample opportunity for participants to reflect on and process new information in light of their background.

- **Adults have a problem-solving orientation.** They want to learn the practical application of general concepts and ideas. As workshop leader you need to articulate the link between theory and practice and focus on practical ideas that address participants' personal concerns.

- **Adults can be a valuable resource for one another.** You can capitalize on the collective expertise of the group by weaving in many opportunities for participants to have discussions with one another, share insights, and solve important problems together.

- **Adults lead busy, frenetic lives.** They may have concerns outside the workshop situation that impact their ability to learn. Participants who juggle multiple responsibilities may be tired by the time they walk through the door of your workshop room. This can affect their ability to concentrate and attend to content. You need to be mindful that the personal, family, work, and community obligations of participants may also affect their ability to follow through.

- **Adults often have fixed viewpoints and entrenched habits.** This means your participants may need to unlearn established behaviors and attitudes before they can learn new ways of thinking and doing things. Like a comfortable pair of old shoes, habits are not easy to give up. You need to be patient and supportive of participants as they struggle to integrate new ideas into old paradigms.

- **Adults are affected by the aging process.** Age affects recall and memory and the length of time it takes participants to master new concepts. It also affects participants' general energy level and ability to concentrate. Participants with lower-back pain or poor circulation will find it difficult to sit for long periods of time. If you are younger than your workshop participants, be particularly sensitive to these issues, and structure the learning environment to accommodate their physical and age-related needs.

- **Adults have a deep need to be self-directing.** They want to be active agents in structuring their learning experiences. The element of choice is critical to successfully working with adults. Adults need to know that they are engaged in a process of mutual inquiry and that the trainer does not view them merely as empty vessels into which knowledge is poured.

- **Adults want to be treated with dignity and respect.** They don't want to be treated like children or asked to do silly or frivolous activities that have no connection to the content of the session. If you patronize your participants or distance yourself from them by flaunting your credentials, you will undermine your goal of empowering them to become lifelong learners.

Addressing and Stretching Learning Styles

Think back to an energizing, high-impact workshop you have attended. No doubt one of the reasons the experience was memorable was that the instructional style of the presenter really clicked with your own style of learning.

I suspect you have also attended a workshop where the content was really important to you, but the experience fell short of your expectations. Learning seemed like real drudgery. It is possible that the presenter's style just didn't mesh with your learning style. Your experience is a prime example that teaching does not guarantee learning.

No matter what or how you teach, learners will respond in diverse ways.

Elizabeth Jones

The term *learning styles* describes the multiple ways that individuals make sense of their world. It includes the diverse ways we decode, encode, process, store, and retrieve information as well as the emotional and environmental elements that affect our motivation and desire to learn. A person's learning style clearly influences his or her receptivity to different instructional strategies and the degree to which concepts are internalized.

During the past three decades, dozens of learning-style models have sprung up in the landscape of educational research. Each seems to have its own inventory and clever way of classifying and interpreting individual variations. A trainer can easily feel overwhelmed and confused by all the descriptors. Worrying whether Kolb, Gregorc, McCarthy, or Barbe is most right is simply unproductive. The specific scheme or classification is less important than understanding that there exists a rich diversity of learners. As a trainer you need to honor that diversity by using a wide repertoire of instructional strategies. Two things to take into consideration are variety and choice.

Variety

Recognizing that there are a variety of learning styles underscores the importance of using a multimodal approach to activate learning. By infusing variety into your presentation, not only do you increase the likelihood of addressing the varied learning styles of your participants, but you also expose participants to new ways of learning that will help them stretch their ways of knowing and doing.

Later in this chapter, as I describe sensory styles, teaching to the whole brain, and multiple intelligences, I've included dozens of ways you can spice up your workshops with activities that address different learning styles. In later chapters you'll also find a collection of interactive exercises that tap different styles of learning. The key is variety — being flexible in your instructional approaches so as to communicate the same content in a rich assortment of ways.

I also think it is important to discuss differences in learning style at the beginning of a workshop. This makes participants more conscious of the ways that they process information and heightens their receptivity to new techniques. I learned this lesson from my colleague, Bernadette Herman, who boldly announces at the beginning of each workshop she conducts, "I guarantee you equal opportunity to experience frustration." She then goes on to describe the different strategies she will be using to accommodate different modes of learning. This not only increases participants' appreciation for the diversity in the group, it makes them more tolerant when she uses an activity or instructional strategy that pulls them out of their learning-style comfort zone.

Choice

Earlier in this chapter, when talking about the principles of adult learning, I stressed that the element of choice is critical to adults. Self-efficacy is increased when adults are empowered to make decisions about their learning that are important to them. The element of choice is also critical when addressing learning styles. Try to structure your workshops to involve participants actively in making choices. For example, when assigning an activity to small groups, you might provide two or three ways the group can complete it, for example giving an oral summary, representing ideas through symbols and pictures, composing a song or skit that captures the essence of their ideas. When you assign a set of questions for different teams to discuss, allow individuals to select the topic that most interests them.

The golden rule is never force participants to engage in activities that may cause them extreme discomfort or embarrassment. Reporting orally before the whole group, for example, can be very stressful for some individuals. Simply asking for volunteers to assume different leadership and reporting roles can help create a climate for full engagement.

If you have contact with participants before to the session, ask for their input on food selections for snack or lunch, on whether they like several short breaks during the day or a couple long ones. During the workshop, provide choice in where they sit, whom they select as learning partners, and freedom to get up and move around and go to the restroom when the need arises. Providing simple choices like these that honor the diverse ways individuals respond to the sociological, physical, and environmental elements of learning can help increase motivation and buy-in.

Tapping the Senses

From birth we take in information about our world through all of our senses — visual, auditory, kinesthetic, olfactory, and taste. We use our senses to make connections between what we know and what we don't know. We also use our senses to express that understanding. Over time each one of us has developed certain preferences or perceptual modality strengths. These strengths dictate how we take in new information and how receptive we are to that information.

In a workshop environment it is the visual, auditory, and kinesthetic senses we tap the most. Some individuals *see* information (by reading and viewing), some *hear* information (by listening), and some *feel* the information (by doing). We also use these same senses to express ourselves, visually through writing and drawing, orally through speaking, and kinesthetically by demonstrating or showing.

It isn't necessary to give people an elaborate inventory to assess their sensory style. Merely asking them to think about how they would like to learn a foreign language or a new sport, how they go about making a decision or solving a problem, and what activities they like to do in their spare time gives you valuable data about their perceptual preferences. Their behavior in your workshop also provides clues as to their sensory style. The "Behavioral Indicators" on the following page provides a summary of things to look for.

Behavioral Indicators

Visual	Auditory	Kinesthetic
Organized	Talks to self	Responds to physical rewards
Neat and orderly	Is easily distracted	Touches people and stands close
Observant	Moves lips, says words when reading	Is physically oriented
Quieter	Can repeat back	Moves a lot
Appearance oriented	Finds spoken language easy	Has larger physical reactions
More deliberate	Finds math and writing difficult	Early large muscle development
A good speller	Speaks in rhythmic pattern	Learns by doing
Memorizes using mind pictures	Likes music	Memorizes by walking, seeing
Less distracted by noise	Can mimic tone, pitch, and timbre	Points when reading
Trouble remembering verbal instructions	Learns by listening	Gestures a lot
Would rather read than be read to	Memorizes by steps, sequence	Responds physically
Voice		
Chin is up, voice high	"Marks off" with tone and tempo	Chin is down, voice louder
Learning		
Needs overall view and purpose and a vision for details; cautious until mentally clear	Dialogues both internally and externally; tries alternatives verbally first	Learns through manipulating and actually doing
Recall		
Remembers what was seen	Remembers what was discussed	Remembers an overall impression of what was experienced
Conversation		
Has to have the whole picture; very detailed	Talkative, loves discussions, may monopolize; has tendency for tangents and telling whole sequential event	Laconic, tactile, uses gestures and movements, uses action words
Spelling		
Most accurate of three modes; actually sees words and can spell them. Confused when spelling words never seen before	Uses phonetic approach, spells with a rhythmic movement	Counts out letters with body movements and checks with internal feelings
Reading		
Strong, successful reader, has speed	Attacks unknown words well, enjoys reading aloud and listening; often slow because of subvocalizing	Likes plot-oriented books, reflects action of story with body movement
Writing		
Having it look OK is important, learning neatness is easy	Tends to talk better than write, and likes to talk when writing	Thick, pressured handwriting that's not as good as others'
Imagination		
Vivid imagery, can see possibilities, details appear; is best mode for long-term planning	Sounds and voices heard	Tends to act the image out; wants to walk through it. Intuitive; weak on details

From Grinder, M. (1991). _Righting the educational conveyer belt._ Portland, OR: Metamorphous Press, pp 20-21. Reprinted with permission.

Visual

Visual learners learn best when information is written out. They prefer diagrams, charts, and tables as learning aids. Visual learners also enjoy media such as films, videos, and pictures. They are the participants who comment on what you are wearing and notice the small details of your outfit, like the

earrings or pin you have chosen as an accessory. When given a choice of where to sit at a workshop, they often sit near the front of the room so they can easily see you and the visuals you use. Visual learners are usually good spellers and can actually see the words in their minds. They like an environment that is visually pleasing, not too distracting or cluttered. They appreciate handouts and will often notice small details like a misspelled word on a transparency. Visual learners have trouble remembering verbal instructions and would rather read than be read to. They like to take notes or doodle during presentations, although there is no guarantee they will refer to these notes once they leave your workshop.

Auditory

Auditory learners learn best by hearing things spoken. They prefer small and large group discussions, lectures, storytelling, and audiotapes as instructional aids. Auditory learners appreciate good speakers. They are able to recall the specifics of what was said as well as how it was said. Auditory learners often

have an inner dialogue going on during a presentation, playing with the pros and cons of an issue to clarify concepts internally. Many auditory learners enjoy music and other auditory stimuli during presentations, but they can also be easily distracted by environmental noises that prevent them from concentrating. Auditory learners are talkative and love discussion. They can sometimes get carried away with lengthy descriptions. They can spell better out loud than when writing out words. Auditory learners may resist exercises that involve visualization and guided imagery.

Kinesthetic

Kinesthetic learners learn best by touching, moving, and feeling. They like to be active and involved in learning new things. They learn best by manipulating objects, acting out scenarios, and playing games. When given a choice, kinesthetic learners sit at the rear of the workshop room so they can stretch out, move around, or get up and go to the restroom

during the session. Kinesthetic learners use action words and gestures when speaking. They enjoy role-playing, dramatizations, games, and any type of activity where they are physically engaged in the learning process. Kinesthetic

Things seen are mightier than things heard

Alfred Lord Tennyson

learners tend to gesture more than visual or auditory learners. They may touch another person to get their attention and use a finger to guide their reading. Variety in action is crucial for kinesthetic learners. They can't sit for long periods of time.

How we engage the senses in our workshops has a clear impact on the retention and recall of important information. The specific amount of information people are able to access from their short- and long-term memory depends on a number of important variables, such as the complexity of information being retrieved, the amount of time that has lapsed, and people's emotional connections to the information. The research is clear, however, that the more senses activated and engaged in the learning process, the greater the likelihood of recall. The "We Remember" pyramid below shows the average percentage of retention after 24 hours for different instructional strategies.

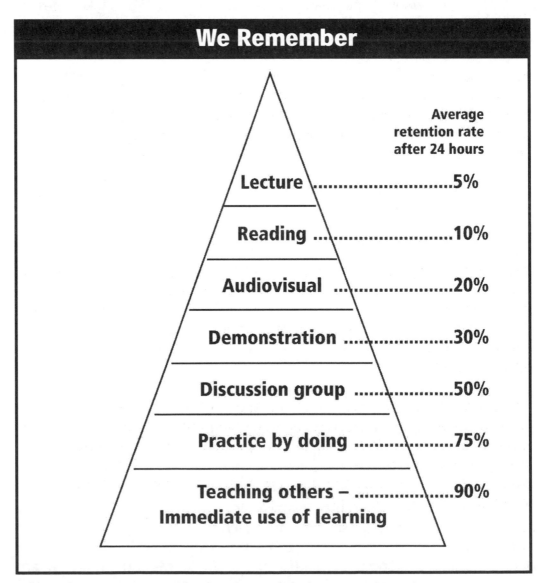

We Remember

Average retention rate after 24 hours

Lecture 5%

Reading 10%

Audiovisual 20%

Demonstration 30%

Discussion group 50%

Practice by doing 75%

Teaching others – 90%
Immediate use of learning

From Sousa D. (1995). How the brain learns. Reston, VA: NASSP. Reprinted with permission.

Teaching to the Whole Brain

The astounding advances in the neurosciences over the past decade have provided us with a scientific basis for effective teaching and learning. Research in the area of whole-brain functioning, in particular, has increased our understanding of how people process and organize information and retrieve it from short- and long-term memory.

Research has also helped us refine the concept of hemispheric specialization, or left-brain and right-brain functioning. While it is true there are fundamental differences in the way information is processed by the two hemispheres of the brain, the emphasis now is on relative laterality and whole-brain strategies for learning instead of differentiating learning strategies by left-brain or right-brain preferences.

People have two ways of processing and organizing information. The left hemisphere specializes in linear, sequential, and analytic operations, whereas the right hemisphere specializes in simultaneous holistic and visual-spatial operations. Processing is simultaneous but sometimes imbalanced. Linear modes of processing and organizing information rely on language and logic. Holistic modes of processing and organizing information rely predominantly on nonverbal, visual, and kinesthetic modes. Because every brain simultaneously perceives and processes parts and wholes, instructional strategies that incorporate both approaches can help us facilitate a higher level of understanding and comprehension in our workshop participants.

What does this mean in practical terms for you as a presenter? It means that traditional modes of instruction through lecture, reading, writing, and discussion are important but may not always help participants connect the known to the unknown in new ways. Most traditional training activities ask participants to think, analyze, and be logical. Only infrequently do we give them permission to tune in to their feelings and emotions and unleash their playful, intuitive, and creative selves — to do what good early childhood educators do best.

Effective workshop presenters look for strategies that help achieve a better balance between the analytic ways of learning and the global and holistic ways of learning. In later chapters I've included a variety of instructional strategies that incorporate metaphor, visualization, art, and music. These are just a few of the strategies you can incorporate into your workshops to reinforce whole-brain learning.

The chief function of your body is to carry your brain around.

Thomas Edison

Engaging the Heart

Learning is not just a cognitive activity. If you are to be effective as a workshop leader, you need to engage the heart as well as the head. In addressing the affective elements of learning style, we make the distinction between the "can-do" aspects of learning — a person's intellectual capacity to grasp new concepts and ideas — and the "wanna-do" aspects of learning — that desire and motivation to attend to and absorb what is going on. The affective aspects of learning style include personality characteristics related to motivation, attention, locus of control, interests, risk taking, persistence, responsibility, and sociability.

It may be easy to get the attention of participants by using surprise and novelty, but sustained attention and real mental engagement require buy-in to the goals of the task. It is also easy to make instructional goals clear to participants by writing them down and verbally reviewing them, but having participants accept and want to work toward the goals is far more problematic.

Recent brain research has shown that attention to and motivation for tasks are complex internal states that are highly dependent on the participants' past experiences and present intentions. This is why asking participants their most memorable experiences about a specific topic is so meaningful. Such connections can be highly charged and emotional, especially if you listen and reflect on what is being said.

Even when learning goals are agreed upon, there may be psychological barriers to engagement. Participants bring to each workshop a whole emotional history of experiences related to school and learning. Some of these memories are positive, some are negative. For example, past experiences in which teachers were perceived as authority figures and individuals were expected to listen passively, take notes, memorize, and regurgitate content may affect participants' attitudes toward you and the learning experiences you have planned. Some participants who attend your workshops may harbor deep insecurities about their abilities. They fear being called on lest they give the "wrong" answer. They may even sit in the back of the room and not make eye contact, hoping to blend in with the walls.

Robert Kegan warns us that educators seeking self-direction from adult learners are not merely asking them to take on new skills, modify their learning style, or increase their self-confidence. They are asking many of them to change the way they understand themselves, their world, and the relationship between the two.

Determining participants' feelings — their fears, their preoccupations, and their attitudes about you as the trainer and about the topic of your presentation — is essential for planning a successful learning experience. If you have contact with participants before the workshop, determining some of these issues may be done as part of a needs assessment. If you are going to be meeting the participants for the first time the day of the workshop session, you should include some initial activity to help you assess their concerns and personal expectations; otherwise you will be stumbling in the dark. In Chapters 6 and 7 we'll address these issues in greater depth.

Celebrating Multiple Intelligences

The theory of multiple intelligences espoused by Howard Gardner provides yet another way to understand the rich diversity of learners who attend your workshops. Gardner believes that intelligence is the ability to respond successfully to new situations and the capacity to learn from past experiences. While learning styles describe how individuals engage in problem solving, multiple intelligences focus on individuals' problem-solving pathways.

Gardner proposes eight kinds of intelligence: verbal-linguistic, logical-mathematical, rhythmic-musical, visual-spatial, bodily-kinesthetic, interpersonal, intrapersonal, and naturalistic. The table "Supporting Multiple Intelligences" summarizes the processing operations associated with each of these intelligences and some instructional strategies that tap these operations.

When you support adults' individual abilities and build on their multiple intelligences, you reinforce the principle that there are multiple ways to learn and multiple ways to show what each person has learned. Teaching to multiple intelligences is on the cutting edge of common sense. Such an approach expands the modes of information processing and provides flexibility for participants to move into and out of various modes of learning.

What lies behind us and what lies before us are small matters compared with what lies within us.

Ralph Waldo Emerson

Intelligence is the human ability to solve problems or make something that is valued in one or more cultural settings.

Howard Gardner

Supporting Multiple Intelligences

Intelligence	Processing Operations	Instructional Strategies
Verbal-linguistic	Sensitivity to sounds, rhythms, poetry, journal writing, storytelling, speeches, concept maps, discussions, brainteasers, puns, riddles, crossword puzzles, word games, choral reading	Lectures, debates, talk shows, interviews, poetry, journal writing, storytelling, speeches, concept maps, discussions, brainteasers, puns, riddles, crossword puzzles, word games, choral reading
Logical-mathematical	Sensitivity to, and capacity to detect, logical or numerical patterns; ability to handle long chains of logical reasoning	Computation, brainteasers, sequencing, outlining, experimentation, charts, venn diagrams, rank ordering, graphic organizers, compare-contrast, cause-effect, time lines, predictions, syllogism, formulas, chunking
Rhythmic-musical	Ability to produce and appreciate pitch, rhythm (or melody), and aesthetic-sounding tones; understanding of the forms of musical expressiveness	Jingles, raps, parodies, phrases, rhythmic beats, nature sounds, humming, rounds, instrumentation, background music, tongue twisters, mood creations, patterning, auditory mnemonics, human orchestra
Visual-spatial	Ability to perceive the visual-spatial world accurately, to perform transformations on those perceptions, and to recreate aspects of visual experience in the absence of relevant stimuli	Visualizations, watching, color sensitivity, highlighting, doodling, drawing, murals, metaphors, collages, sculpting, dioramas, posters, board games, slide shows, mind-mapping, graphic representations, cartooning, mobiles, creative associations, guided imagery
Bodily-kinesthetic	Ability to use the body skillfully for expressive as well as goal-directed purposes; ability to handle objects skillfully	Gestures, role playing, charades, dances, drama, simulations, crafts, constructing, walk-and-talk sharing, task cards, fieldtrips, demonstrations, relaxation exercises, tactile activities
Interpersonal	Ability to detect and respond appropriately to the moods, temperaments, motivations, and intentions of others	Social games, cooperative learning groups, role-playing, discussions, human graphs, peer sharing, teams, meetings, pooling, interviews, panels, round tables
Intrapersonal	Ability to discriminate complex inner feelings and to use them to guide one's own behavior; knowledge of one's own strengths, weaknesses, desires, and intelligences	Meditation, self-talk, journaling, guided imagery, metacognition, autobiographies, analogies, values exploration, self-study, self-assessment, centering, silence, divergent questions, visualization
Naturalistic	Ability to recognize, discriminate, and classify living things as well as sensitivity to other features of the natural world	Observation, environmental tracking, care for living things, photography, classifying nature, cultural artifacts, pattern recognition, ecology projects, restoration projects

Adapted from Herman, B. (1999). Teach me - Reach me! Deerfield, IL: Pathways to Learning and Armstrong, T. (1994). Multiple intelligences in the classroom. Alexandria, VA: ASCD.

Four Types of Learners

The work of Anthony Gregorc provides a useful framework for thinking about the different types of learners who attend your workshops. He proposes that there are two ways individuals perceive information — concretely and abstractly — and two ways they process and organize information — sequentially and randomly. Although everyone uses all these perceptual and processing modes to some degree, the unique combinations of where people fall on these two intersecting continua create unique learning styles.

For the sake of our discussion, I refer to people as practical learners, analytic learners, imaginative learners, and inventive learners. This is not to imply that every participant in your workshops will fall conveniently into one of these four categories. To the contrary, most people embody a combination of these styles. The typologies are useful, however, because if you plan a workshop to address and stretch these four styles, you will have achieved a well-balanced approach in your instructional style.

If we were all alike, we'd only need one of us.

Lilian Katz

Practical learners

More than anything else, practical learners want to see the real-life application of the ideas you present. Their favorite question is, "How can I use this?" They learn through direct experience and want tangible evidence of learning in the form of handouts, products, notes, and recipes. It is important for practical learners to have a sense of where they are going and what you hope to accomplish during the workshop, so a detailed agenda and periodic updates on your progress are essential. They get impatient when other participants ramble or stray from the point.

Practical learners strive for perfection, so they will press you for the one right answer. Depending on the discussion, it may be important to resist the temptation to give one. They are interested in facts and details, so step-by-step directions are essential. Sometimes practical learners are so busy looking at the details, they miss the big picture. These participants work well within time limits, but closure is important to them. As often as possible, avoid running out of time or cutting off discussion prematurely, or else acknowledge that the discussion defies closure.

Analytic learners

Analyzers weigh the pros and cons, advantages and disadvantages, and good and bad of each issue presented in your workshop. They are interested in  your credentials as a presenter and want a trainer who is an expert on the subject. They are often verbal participants — the ones tossing out the hard questions and challenging you for your rationale, the logic, or the research backing your statements. Their favorite question is, "How do you know this is true?" They live in the world of abstract ideas, see the big picture, and enjoy analyzing every angle of a situation. They use facts to prove or disprove their theories.

Analyzers are quite content to sit through lectures as long as they have an opportunity for vigorous debate and discussion following your presentation. Analytic learners can be indecisive. Analytic learners come to workshops to hear the expert, so they may be impatient with cooperative learning strategies or activities where participants process information in small groups. They do not consider participant-to-participant interactions to be as as important as presenter-to-participant interactions.

Imaginative learners

Imaginative learners are the people-people who come to your workshops. They wear their hearts on their sleeves and focus on the processes of the workshop more than the content. For them, learning must be personalized; their emotions influence their ability to concentrate. It is essential with imaginative learners to tend to their emotional, social, and physical needs. They thrive on personal meaning and personal involvement in workshops. They also recognize the emotional needs of others. Their favorite question is, "Why is this important?" They want to know how they can make a difference. Time is irrelevant to imaginative learners; they may not complete exercises or return from breaks on time. Small group discussions and in-depth sharing with a learning partner are favorite instructional strategies with these participants. Imaginative learners need a lot of time to reflect and process ideas. They often engage in flights of fantasy, sprinkle their conversation with superlatives, and focus on the big picture with the risk of missing the details.

Inventive learners

Inventive learners need a lot of mental elbowroom in workshops. They use experimentation as well as their insights and instincts to solve problems. Inventive learners make intuitive leaps and take risks to come up with new and novel ways to solve problems. They might test poorly because they think too much about the nuances of questions. Inventive learners need flexibility in instructional strategies so they can create innovative spin-offs. In your workshops they'll contribute many creative ideas and inspire others to take action. Their favorite question is "What if...?" While inventive learners are inquisitive and independent learners, they can also be impulsive. They think fast on their feet. Don't be discouraged if they don't follow directions exactly; they need room to come up with alternative paradigms.

In the table "Four Types of Learners" on the following page, you can see why a wide repertoire of instructional strategies is essential if you are going to meet the needs of these four types of learners. Some participants want to listen to your ideas; others want to try them out. Some enjoy discussing issues; other want to discover them for themselves. Diversity in your approach is the key.

Four Types of Learners

Their Comfort Zone	Their Frustration Zone	Instructional Strategies for Leaders
Practical Learners		
Learns through senses, direct experience, models, manipulatives, practice, ordering, patterning, logic, and facts. Wants direct practical payoff. Is task oriented and gives attention to detail. Likes time limits and deadlines; needs closure.	May get frustrated with tasks requiring divergent thinking, unexpected changes, too many choices, loose structure, conflicting data, or open-ended requirements.	Use samples, visuals, charts, note-taking guides, advance organizers, outlining, time lines, self-correcting activities, and situational how-to's. Incorporate hands-on activities such as puzzles, manipulatives, task cards, and constructions.
Analytic Learners		
Learns through the exploration of ideas using comparison-contrast and weighing pros and cons. Relies on facts and logic. Analyzes various angles and seeks evaluative feedback. Gives attention to larger picture.	May get frustrated with divergent strategies with no obvious relevance to task at hand. Doesn't like picky and apparently unrelated details or expectations. Dislikes activities that deal with emotions.	Teach through lectures, brainteasers, readings, surfing the net, debates, and independent work. Provide privacy to think through "why" questions. Provide opportunities to analyze and discuss merits of different issues.
Imaginative Learners		
Learns through sixth sense, from people and surroundings. Is reflective and flexible in thinking. Highly imaginative, sensitive, and attuned to emotions. Sees global picture.	May get frustrated by rote memory and tasks, outlining, organizing, deadlines and pressures about time. Doesn't like detail-oriented tasks requiring precision and concentration.	Provide group discussion and one-on-one peer sharing. Give time to explore and generate possibilities. Use color, images, visuals, fantasy, and role play. Stress personalized applications.
Inventive Learners		
Learns through intuitive leaps, experimentation, and creative endeavors. Seeks alternatives and takes risks. Visualizes the future and creates change. Is curious and invents unusual solutions.	May have difficulty meeting deadlines and following specific procedures. Frustrated with tasks requiring detailed notetaking, choosing one answer, ordering and prioritizing, or requiring linear input.	Use open-ended questions and tasks, trial and error, and choices with room for independence and creativity. Stress application to real world, metaphors, inventions, explorations, and problem solving.

Adapted from Herman, B. (1999). Teach me - Reach me! Deerfield, IL: Pathways to Learning and Tobias, C. (1994). The way they learn. Colorado Springs, CO: Focus on the Family Publishing.

Setting the Stage for Success — Workshop Design

Any workshop you give, regardless of how short, deserves thoughtful planning. A haphazard approach to training not only wastes the time of participants, it hurts your reputation. A well-designed workshop will give you the confidence you need on the day of your presentation to focus on the needs of your participants. If you are still scrambling around at the last minute trying to organize your ideas, run off handouts, and prepare visuals, you'll be a nervous wreck by the time you open your mouth. You'll also risk coming across as disorganized and incompetent. A bit of planning can prevent this.

First-class workshops flow with such ease that to the casual observer they appear quite unstructured. Underlying that flow, however, is a well-planned structure. This chapter walks you through the steps of designing your workshop, from determining the scope and goals of your session to organizing your ideas and planning your time. Here are some of the questions you can ask yourself as you move through the process of translating your ideas into a well-crafted presentation.

- ✔ After participants complete this workshop, what do I want them to know, be able to do, and think about?
- ✔ How does this training experience fit into the larger context of participants' professional development experiences?
- ✔ What are the key concepts I want to communicate?
- ✔ What specific instructional strategies can I use to maximize learning?
- ✔ How can I structure the time, physical space, and materials to support my learning goals?
- ✔ What will be the indicators of success for this workshop?

Before we leap into the specifics of planning your workshop, it might be helpful to review some basic principles of the learning cycle. These principles will serve as the foundation for your planning activities.

The Learning Cycle

Workshops grounded in a constructivist philosophy of how individuals learn new information and internalize meaning begin with the premise that participants are not passive recipients of our wisdom, but rather active agents in constructing new knowledge. They do this by connecting their current understanding and experiences to new information and ideas. There are three important phases in the learning cycle that can serve as a systematic framework for planning your workshop: (1) making connections with prior learning, (2) making connections with new knowledge, and (3) making connections with possible applications.

Phase 1: Making connections with prior learning

This first phase of the learning cycle underscores the essential point that existing knowledge and experiences are the foundation for new learning. If you can introduce new information in such a way that it builds on experience or knowledge already gained, then participants can assimilate new material much more easily. Acknowledge participants' familiarity with a concept when you introduce it, and incorporate strategies to help them recall previously learned information.

In their book *Training Teachers*, Margie Carter and Deb Curtis talk about using childhood memories as a strategy for connecting with previous knowledge and experiences. My colleague Chip Donohue does this skillfully in a workshop he conducts on designing outdoor learning environments. He has participants think back to their favorite outdoor places to play as a child. He evokes emotional and sensory connections as he asks them to describe the elements of a joyful play environment, one that invites exploration and discovery, peaks curiosity, and engages the child totally in the play experience.

Helping participants get in touch with what they already know sets the stage for new learning. Activities like brainstorming, identifying, listing, charting, visualizing, and sorting are particularly good instructional strategies to use to support this type of associative thinking.

Phase 2: Making connections with new knowledge

In the second phase of the learning cycle, new information is introduced and participants learn new vocabulary, test hypotheses, practice new skills, and construct mental models for understanding concepts and theories. As new information is considered, new questions are raised. Instructional strategies during Phase 3 can be as varied as lecture, demonstrations, small and large group discussions, interviewing, and interactive games.

In this phase of the learning cycle of Chip's outdoor environmental design workshop, he introduces participants to American's with Disabilities playground safety laws and regulations, playground design options, and resources for landscaping outdoor environments. As participants construct model designs and evaluate the effectiveness of the designs using group-generated criteria, new information is shared and new questions raised.

Phase 3: Making connections to new applications

After exposure to new information, participants are ready to make the leap to the application phase of the learning cycle. This is where many workshops short-circuit the learning process. They spend ample time introducing participants to new concepts and ideas but give scant attention to how that information can be integrated into previous frameworks of knowledge, skills, and behaviors so it can be applied in the future. The activities that take place in this phase of the learning cycle are critical to the consolidation of knowledge into new ways of thinking and behaving.

Your role is crucial in helping participants reframe new information in light of their previous conceptualizations, ideas, and experiences. During Phase 3 of the learning cycle, concepts move from the abstract to the concrete. Participants are challenged to synthesize meaning, make generalizations, draw conclusions, and apply their learning to new situations. Inconsistencies between their previous notions and new data are uncovered and confronted. Your job is to help participants negotiate this disequilibrium.

Because learning is constructed both personally and socially, it is important that time set aside for individual reflection, journaling, and developing action plans be balanced with public discussion and group processing. The sharing of new insights, questions, concerns, and personal contradictions can help participants serve as a rich resource for one another in supporting continued exploration of the ideas when they leave the workshop environment. It also reinforces your larger goal of helping participants work effectively together as members of a learning community.

Chip's environmental design workshop devotes considerable time for this phase of the learning cycle. He structures activities so that participants can apply their new concepts to an action plan for upgrading their outdoor play

Teaching is not pleasing people. It is opening them to possibilities.

Sharon Stine

environments. Participants work first individually and then in small groups, providing feedback to one another on proposed ideas. Small groups then share their designs with the whole group. Participants leave the workshop not only enlightened and empowered by the new ideas and concepts they have learned, but energized and enthusiastic about applying those ideas at their respective child care centers.

Steps in Planning a Workshop

Think of your workshop as an airplane trip in which you are pilot, navigator, and flight attendant all wrapped up in one. You wouldn't think of taking off for a trip to Omaha without a clear flight plan and an understanding of the prevailing conditions along the way. Before taking off, you do a last minute check with passengers to make sure they're all on the right flight and let them know the route you are taking and the anticipated flight time. After a smooth take-off, you provide passengers with food, in-flight entertainment, and periodic updates on the flight's progress. While you've got your flight plan close at hand, you prepare to make midcourse corrections along the way should weather or air traffic conditions change. You let your passengers know when you are about to land, and right on schedule you touch down at your destination.

While a flight to Omaha won't generate the thunderous applause you will after giving your workshop, the airplane analogy is a good one — a successful flight and a successful workshop both take a great deal of planning and coordination. Let's break down the design task into four steps.

Step 1: Determine your objectives

Every good workshop starts out with a clear understanding of what you want to accomplish. In other words, why are you giving this workshop? Your workshop objectives will vary depending on the experience and educational background of the participants, the time allotted for the training, and whether the experience is part of a larger training design.

Your workshop may focus on reinforcing dispositions, teaching new content, acquiring new skills, or sparking enthusiasm for taking on new roles and behaviors. To determine your aims, ask yourself, "What do I want people to know, feel, and do as a result of this training?"

I think a straightforward way to approach this task is to break down your objectives into three categories: knowledge, skills, and attitudes. In the knowledge category list the key concepts, ideas, and theories you want participants to grasp as a result of attending your workshop. These knowledge objectives can be written with varying degrees of specificity using action verbs as stems, such as *to understand, to describe, to identify, to explain, to compare and contrast, to analyze, to recall.*

In the skill category, list the specific new behaviors or skill competencies you want participants to master as a result of attending your workshop. When writing objectives in this category, try to use terms that are measurable and show a relative increase or a relative decrease in something, indicating an improvement achieved. In noting these behavioral objectives use action words such as *to demonstrate, to use, to plan, to develop, to change, to relate, to show, to apply.*

Workshops in which participants learn new skills need to include plenty of opportunity for participants to practice the new behaviors as part of the workshop or ensure that follow-up is provided. The retention rate from workshops is dismal. You can't assume your high-powered performance will be enough to convince people to adopt new practices once they are out from under your spell. Ample practice in the workshop setting or a systematic plan for follow-up is essential if you hope to achieve change in the skill/behavioral category.

Attitude objectives are more difficult to state (and measure) because they relate to participants' beliefs, values, dispositions, and emotional responses. Our attitudes provide evidence of what we deem good, bad, worthy, or unworthy. Objectives relating to attitudes are essential, however, if the purpose of your workshop is to offer opportunities for participants to challenge their assumptions about different issues and embrace new ideas and thought patterns that will result in change.

I believe most presenters are much too ambitious in their workshop goals and objectives. They try to accomplish far more than what can be absorbed by participants in a short block of time. A narrow topic more thoroughly treated can be a far more effective design strategy than a broad topic that receives only cursory attention. Workshops are intensive learning experiences. Feelings of being overwhelmed are not uncommon among workshop participants. This can result in cynicism and a lack of motivation to apply the concepts and information you have taught them in their work setting. Participants may need less information, not more, to jumpstart the application of new knowledge.

Step 2: Determine your content and the sequence of your ideas

Once you have a sense of the objectives you want to accomplish, you can roll into action organizing the content for your workshop. The amount of time allocated to your session, the educational levels of participants, and their familiarity with your topic dictate the breadth and depth of the content you can cover. As you make decisions about key ideas to include, ask yourself, "Why do the participants need to know this information?" This simple question will help you discern the most important items to cover and those that are less important.

The common mistake that new presenters make is trying to cover too much content in the time allotted for their workshop session. They want to share all they know about the topic and don't know how to prioritize those items or key concepts that are most essential. Information overload is the result. Ask yourself what the three or four most important ideas are that you want participants to remember a year after your workshop. Then think about subtopics that can reinforce those key concepts. Above all, keep the amount of content in the workshop realistic.

Putting the content you want into a useable format is not easy. Create a flexible outline by writing your main topics and subtopics on large Post-it Notes. Arrange and rearrange these on a table so that the information and sequence of ideas flows from abstract to concrete and from general to specific. Remember, in effective presentations the pattern of organization is crystal clear to participants. There should be a logical and clear reason why one idea or concept follows another.

After you have decided on the content and sequence of key ideas for your workshop, think about how you might frame the information so that participants can organize and retrieve it easily. Mental models provide the structure or framework for learning to take place. Think about the kind of mental models you can construct to communicate your key concepts. If the mental models you create are truly memorable, participants will be able to retrieve important information for a lifetime.

Step 3: Decide on your instructional strategies

When you have decided on the key topics and subtopics you want to cover, determine the kinds of instructional strategies that will help you communicate the information so that participants can internalize it. Without appropriate instructional strategies, the content you hope to communicate will be lost.

Consider whether your workshop content supports opportunities for humor and fun by using playful icebreakers, openers, art, music, puzzles, games, exercises, and interactive activities or opportunities for more serious reflective instructional modes using learning partners and small group discussion, brainstorming, and role playing. The possibilities are endless, but take special care to select strategies that are appropriate for the tone and content of the topic of your workshop. You wouldn't want to crack jokes or play games that generated a lot of laughter if the topic of your workshop was on helping children deal with death and divorce. Throughout this book you will find dozens of instructional strategies from which to choose.

The guiding principle for determining appropriate instructional strategies is to plan the sequence of your workshop so you present one idea at a time and provide participants with an opportunity to process the information. While people can listen with understanding for about ninety minutes, they can only listen with retention for about twenty minutes. That means if participants are to internalize the information you feel is important, they need an opportunity to think about, question, review, try out, and react to the ideas presented. Too much information without time for processing and reflection is the surest way to create workshop fatigue.

Here is rule of thumb I follow: for every twenty minutes of information I present through more structured approaches like lecture, demonstration, or video, I allow five to ten minutes of processing and reflection time. The formula doesn't always work out precisely, but the key principle I strive for is balance between content and process.

In general, your opening and closing should each take no more than 10% of your allotted time, with the remaining 80% devoted to the body of your workshop. For a one-hour workshop, Margie Carter and Deb Curtis recommend the following break-down of time: welcome, introduction, and overview, 5-10 minutes; opening activity to reflect on topic, 10 minutes; presentation of core ideas, 10-15 minutes; practice applying ideas, 15-20 minutes; next steps and follow-up, 5 minutes; summary and evaluation, 5 minutes.

Bob Garmston recommends that no more than five important facts be presented before participants have a chance to process the information. For less fact-intensive content, processing time might be planned to occur at regular 15-20 minute intervals. Bob Pike has a 90/20/8 rule: no module he teaches ever runs more than ninety minutes, the pace is changed at least every twenty minutes, and he tries to involve people actively in the content every eight minutes.

Some things to keep in mind as you plan your instructional strategies:

- **Provide advance organizers.** Tell people where you are going, and where you have been. Review often.

- **Tap all sensory modes.** Be sure to accommodate visual, auditory, and kinesthetic perceptual modalities when teaching new concepts and skills.

- **Be specific.** Use specific, concrete examples and models to make abstractions and generalizations clear.

- **Vary your instructional strategies.** Don't overuse one type of strategy in a single session.

- **Think about the energy level of the group.** Plan activities to reflect the energy level of people at different times of the day. For example, you'll want to schedule more energizing activities for involvement and movement in the afternoon.

- **Schedule enough breaks.** People need to stretch and move around. You can do this by providing short five- to ten-minute breaks every hour, or longer thirty-minute breaks every one to two hours of instruction.

Step 4: Decide on appropriate visuals aids

For each main idea you present, think about using visual aids that can help clarify the information you are covering. Your visual aids can include handouts, flip charts, transparencies, videos, slides, and a variety of props. Visual aids make content come alive for the visual learners in your workshop. Visual aids are also important to use because they add variety to a presentation and take the focus off of you the presenter. In Chapter 10 you'll find suggestions for designing eye-catching visuals that will enliven your workshop.

Putting It All Together — The Workshop Design Matrix

Once you have done a preliminary outline of your ideas, selected appropriate instructional strategies, and decided on possible visuals, you are ready to put your workshop on paper in a design matrix. Creating a design matrix allows you to see at a glance the overall structure of your workshop and the degree to which you have balanced content and process.

By examining your workshop design matrix, you'll be able to get a good sense of how the workshop will unfold from the participants' perspective. You'll also be able to see if you have enough time to organize your materials for different activities and regroup participants for smooth transitions. Most important, you'll be able to see if the variety of experiential learning strategies you have planned achieves your goal of creating a learning experience that is learner-centered rather than teacher-centered.

Appendix B contains a form you can use to create your own design matrix for an upcoming workshop. As you examine the draft of your completed design matrix, check to see whether you can achieve a greater impact by switching the order of certain activities. For example, showing a video after lunch can be deadly; a dark room may put your participants to sleep. Showing the video immediately before lunch, however, can stimulate discussion of the content of the video during the lunch break.

Finally, examine your design matrix to see if you've built enough flexibility into the flow and sequence of your content and activities. Make sure you've structured the pace to maintain momentum and keep the session lively. This can happen only if you have a well-thought-out structure. But don't let the structure stifle your spontaneity. You certainly want to be flexible enough to respond to those teachable moments that occur in any workshop. A balance between structure and flexibility is essential.

The "Workshop Design Matrix" on the following page is an adaptation of the workshop outline in the Trainer's Guide for *Circle of Influence: Implementing Shared Decision Making and Participative Management*.

Workshop Design Matrix

Circle of Influence
Implementing Shared Decision Making and Participative Management

Time	Topic	Description	Method	Visual Aids
8:30-8:40	Welcome	Introduction, review housekeeping details, announcements		Transparency
8:40-8:50	Workshop goals and objectives	Elicit expectations from the group, review learning outcomes, go over agenda, and establish ground rules	Whole group	Transparencies Handout
8:50-9:00	Icebreaker	Activity: *The Best Decision I Ever Made*	Whole group	Transparency
9:00-9:30	Different roles lead to different perceptions	Activity: *Think About...*	Individual, dyads, whole group	Transparencies Handouts
9:30-10:00	What is participative management?	Activity: *What is Participative Management?* An overview of the principles of collaboration	Lecturette, whole group, small group	Transparencies Flip chart
10:00-10:30	BREAK			
10:30-11:15	Perceptions of power and influence	Activity: *Looking Within* Assessing decision-making style and work style	Individual, lecturette, whole group	Transparencies Handout, props Flip chart
11:15-12:00	A framework for shared decision making	Activity: *Four Questions* Stakeholders, types of decisions, levels of participation, and external constraints	Individual, dyads, lecturette	Transparencies Handout
12:00-1:00	LUNCH			
1:00-2:00	Getting started	Activity: *Creating a Supportive Environment* The director's role in establishing norms of collaboration	Whole group, small group	Flip chart Transparencies Handouts
2:00-2:15	BREAK			
2:15-3:30	Decision making in action	Activity: *Consensus Building* An opportunity to practice consensus decision making and learn about groupthink	Small group, whole group lecturette	Flip chart Transparencies Handouts
3:30-3:45	BREAK			
3:45-3:55	Wrap-up	Activity: *Sharing the Power* Summarize key concepts	Whole group	Props
3:55-4:00	Workshop evaluation	Distribute evaluation forms and thank participants for attending	Individual	Handout

Adapted from Bloom, P. J. (2000). *Trainer's guide for Circle of Influence*. Lake Forest, IL: New Horizons.

Organizing Your Notes

How you organize your notes for your workshop depends on your personal preferences. Some presenters like to work from 4 x 6 or 5 x 7 inch index cards with separate content ideas and corresponding instructional strategies noted on each card. For new presenters this method is good because you can hold your note cards while you talk and refer to them as needed. You can also indicate on your notes when to use different visual aids.

The important point about notes is to make sure they are a help, not a hindrance. Print large enough so you don't have to squint when you refer to them quickly. Also, don't try to cram too much information on each card. Remember, your notes are memory joggers. Use single words, short phrases, or symbols to remind you of each key idea you want to communicate. Avoid the temptation to write out whole sentences. If you have a tendency to talk too fast or in a low voice, you can add occasional reminders to slow down or talk louder, depending on the case. Oh yes, don't forget to number your cards — accidents do happen!

My preference for organizing notes is to do them on the computer and keep them in a three-ring binder. I like this method because my notes are already in the computer and I can update them easily when I read new information about the key concepts or ideas included in my workshop. For cues I can use a large font with bold or underline words. Interspersed in my content notes are recommended instructional strategies and directions for different activities to reinforce key points. I have a place in the margins where I keep comments about what worked well and what didn't, anecdotes to weave in, and humorous quips and quotes to remember.

I put my design matrix and workshop agenda in the front of the binder for easy reference or out on the presenter's table if space permits. I keep my transparencies in a separate folder where I can access them quickly and return them after use so they stay ordered for the next presentation.

While a good workshop is planned, it should not come across as scripted. Highlight key words in your notes to trigger your thoughts about the organization of your ideas. You can also use your flip chart, transparencies, and other visual aids in the room as prompters to help you keep on track. More about this later.

Room Setup and Other Logistics

Presenters don't always have a choice about where and when to deliver their workshops. Workshop leaders who present at local, state, and national conferences, for example, are often at the mercy of conference planners about the logistics of when and where their session is scheduled. They may not even have access to the training room before the session if the conference program has workshops scheduled one right after another using that space.

There will be many times, however, when you will be in the driver's seat, making decisions about the training schedule, room setup, and ambiance. Never take the room for granted. Even the most wonderful workshop can be torture in the wrong room. The tips and ideas in this chapter give you the information to make wise decisions about how your workshop space and logistics can help support your training goals.

Three Questions to Consider

The setup of your training space can have a profound impact on the success of your workshop. You'll want a room with ample space for people to maneuver and move about, yet not so large that you can't achieve the intimacy in connections so important for group dynamics. Your decisions about room setup will be dictated by your answers to the following three questions: How many participants do you anticipate will be attending your workshop? What is the time frame for your workshop? And what instructional strategies do you anticipate using during your session?

How many participants will be attending?

The size of the group attending your workshop is a key determinant in room setup decisions. Small groups (7 to 15 participants) and medium-size groups (15 to 40 participants) give you maximum flexibility in organizing the space, allowing you to arrange tables and chairs in a number of different configurations. With groups of up to 40 participants, you can use flip charts and feel confident that everyone in the room will be able to see. With small and medium-size groups, you can probably get by without a microphone and not have to worry about acoustical problems. With large groups (40 to 100+

participants), however, you have fewer options. You may not be able to use flip charts and you may not be able to guarantee that participants will have a writing surface. You will probably need to be wired to a microphone.

For most workshops, allow a minimum of 20 square feet of space per person. If your workshops are highly interactive, plan on more space. For workshops lasting more than four hours, I try to reserve rooms so I have about 35 square feet per person. Arrange the tables and chairs to allow ample space between rows and to allow people to maneuver around easily without bumping into each other. It is important that you be able to circulate easily around the room.

Unless people have preregistered for your workshop session and you are certain about the actual number of attendees, put out only three-quarters of the chairs you think you'll need. Stack the remaining chairs in the back of the room. If you are using tables, don't put chairs around the tables in the very back of the room. This forces participants who arrive early to take seats up front. Just before you begin your session, add a few additional chairs to the remaining tables for latecomers. This way latecomers won't disturb the session.

What is the time frame for the workshop?

The length of the workshop also affects the room arrangement decisions. If the workshop is under two hours, participants will probably be able to endure almost anything — even sitting on metal chairs and balancing their materials on their laps. If your workshop spans several days, however, pay careful attention to room setup. Consider the psychological impact of spending a whole day or several days in confined quarters. Make sure you have enough room that people won't feel claustrophobic. For workshops longer than four hours, make sure you have sufficient table space for your primary activities as well as extra space for storing belongings or displaying completed projects and resource materials.

What instructional strategies will you be using?

Your choice of instructional strategies clearly will dictate some room arrangement logistics. If you plan to use visuals like overhead transparencies or slides, you'll need to place the screen so everyone can easily see the projected images. If you plan to have participants meet in small groups, you'll want to be able to rearrange chairs quickly or have preset table groupings to facilitate discussion. If you plan to incorporate interactive exercises or games requiring large movement, you'll need extra space to accommodate these activities.

Consider using two or more flip charts in your workshop to increase opportunities for visual memory. Two flip charts gives symmetry to the arrangement of space in the front of the room. For medium-size groups, I sometimes set up the room with four flip charts and position myself (or designated recorders) at different stations during the course of the training. This adds variety and changes people's perspective — critical elements in keeping participants alert. It also allows me more flexibility in setting up the work of small groups. Instead of having to tear off and tape flip chart pages on the wall so groups can record their work, participants can use one of the extra flip charts to write on.

Tables are essential if you plan to ask participants to fill out assessment tools, take notes, or complete written exercises. Tables clearly facilitate small group discussions as well. Seating people at round tables in particular gives participants a feeling of being in smaller groups. When you use round tables or position people around square or rectangular tables, be sure that you only position the chairs around two-thirds of the table so that the view of the front of the room is unobstructed and no one has to turn around to see you.

Some Possible Seating Arrangements

The arrangement of tables and chairs in the room communicates strong nonverbal messages to your participants about your expectations for the workshop. In deciding on the appropriate seating arrangement for your session, there are several options from which to choose: theatre style, classroom style, herringbone, U-shaped, V-shaped, rounds, or conference style. There are advantages and disadvantages of each style. Some arrangements are more conducive to small groups; others appropriate for medium or large groups.

Theatre style

This arrangement is good for lecture or for large groups. It allows you to place the greatest number of seats in the smallest space. The disadvantage is that it discourages audience inter-action and doesn't provide participants with a writing surface. If you use a theatre-style seating arrangement, avoid putting an aisle in the middle as this is prime viewing area.

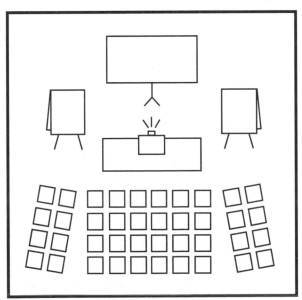

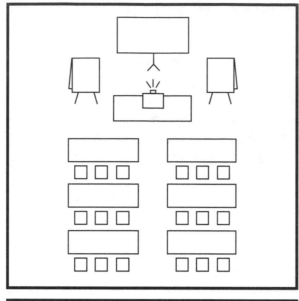

Classroom style

Classroom style is a good arrangement for medium and large groups. It provides a writing surface for participants and focuses attention on the presenter, but it still discourages participant-to-participant interactions. With some adjustments, however, this style can accommodate small group interactions. You can simply ask participants in every other row to turn their chairs around and pair up with the person behind them.

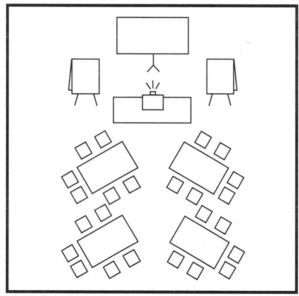

Herringbone style

Herringbone style is a good arrangement for medium-size groups. It has the advantage of providing a writing surface while creating natural clusters for group work. Because participants are angled so they have some view of one another, this arrangement also facilitates participant-to-participant interaction when the group is engaged in discussion.

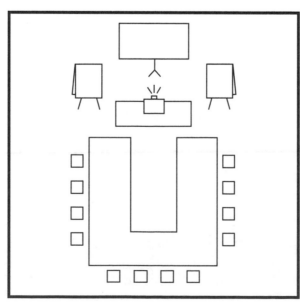

U-shape

The U-shape arrangement is excellent for small groups. It communicates equity in status and encourages interaction among the whole group. The disadvantage of this style is that participants can't see the faces of the people seated on their side of the table.

V-shape

The V-shape arrangement, like the U-shape, is good for small groups. It communicates equity in status but has the advantage that all participants can see one another. It is particularly good for presenter demonstrations or showing overhead transparencies, videos, and slides.

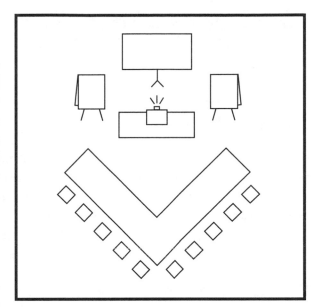

Rounds

Round tables provide a very versatile arrangement for medium and large-size groups. They provide equity in status and natural clusters for small group activities. One of the advantages of this arrangement is that most hotels and conference centers are equipped with round tables and can easily accommodate this room setup request. Don't let the hotel conference planner talk you into putting more than seven or eight chairs at each table, however, or you will defeat your purpose of trying to create a cohesive group dynamic at table clusters.

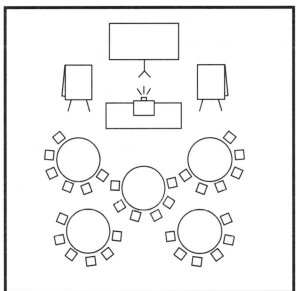

Conference style

Conference style is a good arrangement for small workshops. It accommodates group interaction for problem solving and idea sharing. Like the U-shape arrangement, however, individuals seated on the same side of the table cannot see one another.

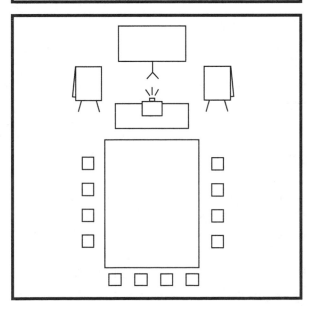

A final thought about seating arrangements. If possible, arrange tables and chairs so that the entrance door is located at the rear of the room. That way people coming in and going out during your workshop will not distract other participants.

Ambiance

No doubt about it, people learn best in pleasant surroundings. The impression people get when they first walk into a workshop can set the tone for an engaging and successful learning experience or dredge up memories of boring educational experiences they have endured. Here are some things to think about in establishing a warm, hospitable atmosphere. They relate to general décor, lighting, temperature and ventilation, and music.

General décor

Try to conduct your training in rooms that have a lot of usable wall space. Before your participants arrive put up a few sheets of flip chart paper decorated with memorable quotes relating to the topic. Add some posters to the room to liven it up. You can give these away as prizes during the training. Masking tape looped on the back of the poster or gummy adhesive will work for tacking these to the wall if push pins are not appropriate.

If your training will stretch over several days, consider bringing in some live or artificial plants to make the workshop space more inviting. I am always amazed by how a bit of greenery can transform a space and alter people's perceptions of the learning experience. If my workshop is close to home, I usually bring a fresh bouquet of flowers to put on the food table. These small touches add elegance to the session and communicate your desire to create a nurturing space for learning.

Position a resource table in the back of the room for displaying materials and setting out handouts for latecomers. This table can also serve as a place where participants can display resources they have brought to share. If available, use table covers or tablecloths on display tables and your presentation table. This is more professional looking and aesthetically pleasing.

If you are conducting your workshop over several days, consider making a photo gallery board on one of the walls, where you can display pictures taken during training. With one-hour photo finishing available at most supermarkets and drugstores these days, it is easy to get photos processed the same day you take them. Participants love this personalized touch. Be sure to have a second set of the photos made to distribute to participants.

Put a caddy of supplies on each table — markers, pens, pencils, Post-it Notes, paperclips, crayons, and extra sheets of paper or writing tablets. For workshops spanning several days, also set up a general supplies table that includes a stapler, scissors, three-hole punch, masking tape, and staple remover.

If the room does not have a wall clock, bring one of your own. I have one of those funny alarm clocks with a big face and hands. I set it on the edge of my presenter's table so everyone can see it easily. That keeps people from having to look down at their watches, and I don't need to refer to my own wristwatch while I am presenting. Occasionally, I even set the alarm to signal time for a break.

Lighting

Considerable research has been conducted on the effects of lighting on people's ability to focus and concentrate. In most cases you do not have control over the kind of lighting available in your training rooms, but you may be able to do some small adjustments that will help ensure a successful learning experience.

In classrooms without natural sunlight, full-spectrum fluorescent lights are a good substitute, but they are more expensive than regular fluorescent lights. Before your session begins, make sure that all fluorescent bulbs are working and none of the bulbs is flickering. You want the room well-lit but not so bright that the lights create a glare. The room should be dark enough for projection, yet light enough for note taking.

If your workshop spans several days, try to schedule your training in a room that has some natural sunlight streaming in. Natural light makes a big difference in the general mood and disposition of a group. If this is not possible, try to make sure that breaks and lunch are held in a place with natural light.

Temperature and ventilation

Temperature and ventilation play a strong role in the general comfort level of participants in a workshop setting. The temperature in a room is affected by the number of participants and the heat emitted from audiovisual equipment.

The length of your session is clearly a determining factor in how assertive you will want to be in having some control over the environmental elements of temperature and ventilation. For a workshop under two hours long, people are usually willing to endure a stuffy, warm room or the hum of an annoying fan. On the other hand, if your workshop spans several days, pay careful attention to temperature and ventilation.

Regulating a thermostat to please all participants is a tricky if not impossible task. Some people are just more cold-blooded than others. One of the most challenging and fun workshops I gave was to a group of middle-age women, many of whom were in the throes of menopause. We played several games over that three-day event, and the winner was designated "Keeper of the Key" — the coveted key that opened the lock to the thermostat box. Each winner wielded great power for her two hours of glory during the course of that workshop.

It is important to read the body language of participants and take their cues about when they may be feeling too cold or too hot. If they start stripping down in the middle of your presentation and folding your handouts into fans, that's a sign that an adjustment in the temperature is in order. It is also important to give participants a choice as to where to sit. Certain seats in the room may get a direct blast from the air conditioning unit, which is appreciated by some participants but not others.

Music

Music affects the emotions, triggering pleasant associations that can affect your participants' learning capacity. Bring your cassette player and tapes along to your workshop session, and play music as participants first enter the room. For workshop openings I generally use something with an upbeat tempo, but the particular selection you use depends on the time of day and the mood you want to create. Music is a great way to set a welcoming tone and transition participants into the learning environment.

Some research supports incorporating music into your repertoire of training strategies. According to Don Campbell in *The Mozart Effect*, Baroque music at sixty beats per minute affects our respiratory system, heart rate, and brainwaves to accelerate learning. The rhythms, melodies, and high frequencies of Mozart's music, he claims, stimulate and charge the creative and motivational regions of the brain. He calls this a kind of sonic Vitamin C. Playing music at periodic points during your workshop can help create a dynamic balance between the more logical left and the more intuitive right hemispheres of the brain — an interplay that may boost creativity.

If you use music, avoid turning it on or off suddenly. Rather, fade in and out slowly. Vary the selections you play. Bring in cassettes or CDs of your favorite jazz, classical, and New Age artists and play them at different times, depending on the mood you want to set. If you are doing a multiday training, invite participants to bring in some of their favorite selections.

You can use music to signal transitions (for example, time to return from a break), as background music for journal writing and guided imagery, or as a way to intensify an air of excitement during humorous interactive games. The key is that music should be incorporated into your training scheme subtly and unobtrusively. If you keep people waiting while you flip through your cassettes to find just the right selection, you will negate the effectiveness of this technique.

Feed 'Em to Please 'Em

In the 1930s, psychologist Gregory Razran conducted a series of experiments using what he called the "luncheon technique." He found when his subjects were being served food, they rated different images of women more favorably. He was even able to reverse previously held biases. Razran's experiments confirm what we all know firsthand — people like food, and people like people who feed them. Participants simply won't focus on the content of your workshop if their physical needs aren't met. If you are planning a workshop more than three hours in length, you need to consider providing some kind of food for participants, if only an energy-boosting snack.

Most workshop trainers tend to defer issues of food to conference planners or coordinating staff at the training facility. I think this is a mistake. When people eat and what they eat can have a profound impact on the success of your workshop. Donuts and coffee for breakfast, lasagna and bread for lunch, cookies and soda for an afternoon snack may be high on the list of your participants' favorites, but the effect of this diet on their ability to learn and have energy throughout the day will be disastrous.

As Judith Wurtman argues in her book *Managing Your Mind and Mood Through Food*, the kind of food we put into our bodies affects alertness, mood, and receptivity to learning. Wurtman presents some cardinal rules for conference menu planning. She says participants feel more energetic, attentive, and motivated if you underfeed them. This doesn't mean starvation rations, but by feeding participants frugally, you help prevent the lethargy and brain drain that results from overeating. Ask your caterer to keep portions modest. Wurtman suggests lunch menus of about 500-600 calories per person and dinner selections (hors d'oeuvres included) of about 600-800 calories per person.

As you plan your menu, be sure to provide some combination of carbohydrate and protein at every meal. For a continental breakfast, instead of serving pastries, donuts, or croissants, ask the caterer to provide bran muffins, yogurt, kefir, juice, and an assortment of fruit. Make regular and decaffeinated coffee available as well as regular and herbal tea.

A chilled salad plate or buffet-style soup-and-salad bar is perfect for lunch if the selections are low fat. If you go with a box lunch, don't forget the vegetarians in your group. Be sure to offer options without meat or poultry. For dessert, ask the deli or caterer to pass on the double fudge brownie and opt for a piece of fresh fruit instead.

For afternoon breaks try to provide some healthy alternatives: fruit, cut-up vegetables and yogurt dip, cheese, crackers, rice cakes, dried fruit and nut mixtures, and juice. Don't forget to make water available throughout the day, with pitchers and glasses on each table or in a convenient location.

If you have some say in where food is located, try to have lunch served in a different location. This ensures a change of scenery and gets people moving around. I like to set an informal tone in my workshops (and also accommodate those kinesthetic learners), so I allow participants to get up any time they want to refill their coffee cups or get a beverage. If you adopt this policy, however, make sure the beverage table is in the very back of the room so the sound of ice clanking into glasses won't disturb others.

Setting Up Your Audiovisual Equipment

The placement of your audiovisual equipment may unfortunately be dictated by factors beyond your control, like the location of electrical outlets in your workshop room or the location of windows and external light sources. I once arrived on the scene of a workshop where I had planned to give a slide

presentation only to find that I had been assigned a classroom with a full bank of windows. The drapes for the windows had been sent to the cleaners (for the first time in 15 years) just two days prior to my workshop. Even with the lights off, it was impossible to show slides. Needless to say, flexibility is the name of the game when it comes to audiovisual equipment. It is always good to have a backup plan.

Projectors

If you plan to use an overhead, LCD, or slide projector as part of your presentation, set up your screen in a location where the projected image can be seen by all participants and where you will not be in the way of the light source. If you get a trapezoidal image (called a *keystone effect*) when you project a light source onto the screen, tilt the screen forward slightly. Also, put the screen up as high as possible. The information at the bottom of the screen is most difficult for the audience to see, so the screen should be set at least 30 inches above the floor.

When you project an image, make sure it fills up the screen. Check that all your transparencies or slides are in focus and that they can be seen from the back of the room. If a light source reflects on the screen, try to dim or disconnect those lights. Also, make sure that natural light streaming in from the windows does not hamper people's viewing of the screen.

Place your overhead projector on a four- or six-foot rectangular table instead of using an audiovisual cart. This table can double as your presenter's table, providing ample room to place your notes, handouts, markers, props, and the transparencies you will be using. Be certain that the projector is not obstructing anyone's view. Tape down cords so you won't have to worry about anyone tripping.

Microphones

For workshops of more than 40 participants, consider using a lavaliere or cordless microphone. That way your hands will be free and you can move around easily. Older participants will especially appreciate it if you use a microphone, so they won't need to strain to hear you.

A microphone is helpful not only because it allows everyone to hear you better, but also because it allows you to augment your message using subtle nuances of your voice to give greater vocal variety to your speech. For long workshops, using a microphone also helps preserve your vocal cords.

Be sure to test the microphone to be certain your voice can be heard in all parts of the room. If you find it gives that ear-splitting feedback when it is turned on or placed too close to the speakers, remedy the situation before your session begins. When you use a microphone, remember to switch it off or remove your lavaliere during breaks or when participants are engaged in small group activities.

The Presenter's Workspace

For workshops spanning several hours to several days, it is important that you establish two workspaces for yourself. The first workspace is your presenter's table. This can be the same table you use for your overhead or LCD projector. A rectangular table two feet wide and four to six feet in length is perfect. On this table you can put the items you will be using during the next hour or two of your presentation — transparencies, handouts, markers, and props.

Your second workspace, your backup table, can be situated behind the projector screen or off to the side in the front of the room. Here you can organize all the extra handouts, transparencies, props, and supplies that you don't need immediately. I sometimes keep my cassette player on my backup table in the very front of the room if a separate audiovisual cart isn't available. Declutter your workspaces as much as possible. If you have organized your materials in labeled boxes, baskets, or Ziploc bags, you can lay them out in the order in which you plan to use them. Your goal is to eliminate visual distractions for the audience and to know mentally exactly where you need to look to retrieve something quickly.

On your presenter's table try to designate a space for markers, masking tape, blank overheads, and other items you use regularly. After use, always return them to that same spot. Some people like to arrange their transparencies housed in translucent sleeves in a three-ring binder. The sleeves can then be removed and placed directly on the overhead projector. This protects the transparency and helps with organization. I have found this method a bit bulky, however, preferring instead to store my transparencies for each segment of my workshop in separate pocket folders. After use, I simply put the used transparency in the other pocket.

Here is a list of things you may want to make sure you have in your presenters' survival kit.

Presenters' Survival Kit

- ❑ Overhead transparencies
- ❑ Blank transparencies
- ❑ Nonpermanent overhead marking pens
- ❑ Water-based flip chart markers (assorted colors)
- ❑ Small clock or timer
- ❑ Extra felt-tip markers for participants
- ❑ Masking tape or drafting tape
- ❑ Push pins
- ❑ Sharpened pencils (one for each participant)
- ❑ Post-it Notes in a variety of sizes and colors
- ❑ Name tent for each person
- ❑ Name tags
- ❑ Chalk
- ❑ Blank paper
- ❑ Extra extension cord
- ❑ Three-prong adaptor
- ❑ Extra Ziploc bags
- ❑ Cassette or CD player and tapes or CDs
- ❑ Scissors
- ❑ 3-hole punch
- ❑ Stapler
- ❑ Safety pins
- ❑ Index cards
- ❑ Paper clips (assorted sizes)
- ❑ Camera and film
- ❑ Anti-static spray
- ❑ Extra pair of nylons (ladies only)
- ❑ Props as needed
- ❑ Aspirin or Tylenol

A Final Checklist of Things To Do

Without a doubt, there will be times when circumstances beyond your control will mean scrambling around at the last minute arranging chairs, posting flip chart pages, or tracking down another extension cord. The unexpected does occur and as a workshop leader, you need to be flexible. To the extent possible, plan your time so that you have at least a full hour for room setup prior to your workshop (longer, of course, if your training is a multiday event). By the time the first participants arrive, you want to have the learning environment completely ready. That way you can give your full attention to greeting and getting to know the attendees before your session begins.

Here are some things to think about as you make your final preparations:

- **Locate light switches.** Know the location of all light switches and familiarize yourself with the dimming controls. Figure out which switch you use to darken the room partially. Find out if you can turn off the lights in the area immediately in front of your screen.

- **Test the overhead projector.** Make sure the bulb is not burned out. Adjust the projected image as needed so it can be seen from every seat in the room. Locate the spare bulb and clean the projection screen.

- **Locate temperature controls.** Know the location of the heating and air-conditioning controls and how to use them.

- **Know whom to contact for technical assistance.** Find out the location of the nearest telephone and the name and number of the individual you can contact in case of an equipment emergency.

- **Check your visuals.** Make sure your transparencies are in their proper sequence and right-side up.

- **Check the flip charts.** Check that there is enough flip chart paper and adjust the positioning of the easel so that the flip chart can be seen by everyone in the room. Tear off one-inch strips of tape and stick them along the side of the easel so they are available when you need them during the workshop.

- **Test the slide projector.** If you are using a slide projector, make sure it is in working condition and that the lens is large enough to project the image size you want. Check that your plastic slide holder fits the projector. Familiarize yourself with how the remote control works.

- **Test the VCR and monitor.** If you are using a VCR and monitor, locate the on/off and volume controls. Insert your videocassette and run it until you arrive at the spot where the film begins.

- **Test all microphones.** If you are using a lavaliere mike, decide where to attach it to your clothing.

- **Check the doors.** Check to see if the doors leading into the room squeak. If they do, call the building engineer to oil the hinges. If the latch on the door makes lots of noise, tape the catch mechanism shut.

- **Locate the nearest restrooms.** Check the location of restrooms, public telephones, and coat check room.

- **Confirm food arrangements.** Review with the caterer the time and location of food for breaks.

I began this chapter by stating that in some training situations you simply don't have a choice about many of the issues relating to room setup or general ambiance. If you are one of a dozen or more presenters conducting a workshop at a state or national conference, you may be lucky to have ten minutes to set up before your session. In such situations, tending to squeaky doors will not be high on your list of last-minute things to do. The amount of time you spend focusing on environmental issues should relate directly to the length of your workshop. Don't drive yourself crazy trying to be the Martha Stewart of workshop ambiance, but do ensure that your room setup supports your goals and isn't an obstacle to learning.

Starting Off on the Right Foot

What happens in the first twenty minutes of your workshop largely determines how productive your session will be. In that brief time, participants are sizing you up as a presenter and making quick assessments about your credibility. They are forming instant impressions about the nature of the learning experience that is about to unfold and deciding on the level of commitment they will give.

There are three things you should communicate to your participants in those opening minutes of your session:

✔ you are excited and confident about the subject matter
✔ you care about each participant as a unique learner
✔ you are well organized and will not waste their time

This chapter provides suggestions for overcoming nervousness, presenting attention-getting openings, and aligning goals for learning. It also covers the basics of the organizational details of your session, such as reviewing the agenda and establishing ground rules. It concludes with a collection of energizing icebreakers and warm-up activities that will help you get your workshop off to a great start.

Overcoming Nervousness

Your palms are sweaty, your throat is parched, your knees are shaking, and the first participant hasn't even arrived. You understand perfectly why fear of presenting in public is so great for some people it ranks ahead of financial troubles, heights, spiders, and deep water. And at this moment you feel like you are the one in over your head.

We all know the signs of nervousness — rapid heartbeat, shortness of breath, butterflies in our stomach — that feeling of being out of control. The thing to remember is that nervousness is a natural state. If you get nervous before (and during) your workshop, you are normal. The trick is to make your nervousness work for you.

Think of your nervousness as a good sign. Your anxiety heightens your awareness of what needs to be done in order to make your workshop a success. Your self-confidence and poise as a speaker depend to a great extent on your ability to relax and be natural under stressful conditions. Anxiety can have an energizing effect and can actually help to improve your performance.

The most important thing to remember is that the participants who have decided to attend your workshop want you to succeed. They have come to engage in a day of discovery and learning. They want to leave feeling their time was well spent. Their goal will be met if your goals are met. They are your allies.

Here are some things you can do to overcome nervousness:

- **Arrive early.** Lack of organization is one of the major causes of anxiety. If you are scrambling around at the last minute trying to get your transparencies in order and track down the electrical outlets in the room, you'll create additional stress. Arrive plenty early so you can organize your materials, run through your notes, and greet the participants. I have found that talking with the participants informally for ten or fifteen minutes before my workshop session begins has a calming effect. It warms me up and reduces any anxiety I might be experiencing.

- **Practice, but don't overprepare.** Walk through your presentation once or twice during the days immediately before your workshop. Practice out loud in front of a mirror if you can, but don't overdo the practicing. If you rehearse too much, you'll be tempted to memorize your talk. That will make you sound too mechanical and lacking in spontaneity. The more extemporaneous a presentation appears to be, the better it goes over. Practice the opening of your workshop the most. If you can get by those first crucial five to ten minutes at the beginning your workshop, the rest will be smooth sailing. Try to fix the sequence of the main points of your content in your mind. As you practice, try to recall ideas, not words.

- **Rehearse using your visual aids.** Trying to recall important points while you are fumbling to focus the overhead projector can cause you to lose concentration. Take some time to rehearse the sequence of using different visuals. This dry run will help you feel more confident on the day of your session. Don't forget that your visual aids can be wonderful prompters to keep you on track and reduce dependency on your notes.

- **Visualize success.** Visualizing helps you to mentally rehearse how your session will unfold. Close your eyes and imagine yourself in the room. Except for your voice, the room is silent. The participants are leaning forward in their chairs listening attentively to your every word. See yourself fielding questions with confidence and enthusiasm. Hear the audience laughing at your jokes. Visualize your closing comments and the participants applauding with appreciation for a job well done. Visualization techniques can be powerful for priming the pump and getting you ready to succeed.

- **Focus on others.** Try not to worry about putting on a good performance. Instead, concentrate on attending to the needs of participants. By shifting your focus from yourself to them, you will automatically reduce the stress that comes with self-consciousness. Imagine yourself in a room with good friends. Try to relate to them as individuals and think about what they need to make the experience an enjoyable and productive one. Taking time before the session to get to know participants one-on-one reduces stress and helps you build audience support. Talking with participants before your session begins also helps you warm up your voice.

- **Concentrate on your breathing.** When you are nervous, your muscles tighten. This constricts the natural flow of oxygen. Consciously concentrate on your breathing by inhaling deeply a number of times. Take full, slow breaths, filling your lungs. Focusing on your breathing patterns will help you clear your mind. Many people also find it helpful to yawn prior to speaking. When you yawn you fill your lungs and relax your throat and vocal chords. You may want to do this when the participants aren't looking, lest they interpret your yawns as a sign of boredom.

- **Do progressive relaxation.** Instead of focusing on the tension in your body, try to focus on relaxing your muscles. Isometric exercises are particularly good in situations like this. Tense and relax different parts of your body. This can release the nervous energy locked in your extremities. Some people also find it helpful to take a brisk walk prior to presenting. It invigorates the spirit and warms the muscles.

The key to overcoming nervousness is to find strategies that work for you. What calms someone else may just make you more uptight. Find your own recipe for tuning into your body and making anxiety an ally instead of an enemy. I know a presenter who keeps a photograph of her piano in her workshop notes. When she looks at the picture of her piano, she is able to call up the same calm, controlled feeling she has when she plays her piano for her family and friends. While public speaking demands a different set of skills from those for playing the piano, she has found that the focused concentration required for piano playing is the same state of mind she needs when conducting a workshop.

The other point to remember is that your nervousness doesn't show nearly as much as it feels. This is because anxiety and stress are largely internal states. Your audience doesn't see what you are experiencing inside. Even if your hands are trembling a bit and your voice quavers some, the audience really doesn't care. What they do care about is that you have a passion for your topic, that you are genuinely interested in them, and that they learn something worthwhile.

Energizing Openings

You can assume your participants have come to your workshop with positive expectations. These expectations can be reinforced or undermined, depending upon how you present yourself in the first few minutes. Your opening sets the tone for your entire workshop, so it is essential you start off on the right foot.

Try your best to start on time. If you wait for stragglers to arrive, you'll be reinforcing the notion that it is all right to be late. This shows a lack of respect for those who arrive on time. If the participants know you start precisely on schedule, they'll also tend to be more prompt returning from breaks.

The length of your opening depends, of course on the length of your workshop, but in general it should not exceed five to ten minutes. Your goal in the introduction is to break the participants' preoccupation with whatever they were thinking about while driving to your session, finding a parking spot, locating the workshop room, and getting settled.

In your opening you want to accomplish three things:

✔ arouse curiosity and get participants excited about the topic
✔ clarify the purpose of the presentation
✔ establish an association the participants have with the content to be presented

The mind is like a parachute; it only works when it is open.

Your opening needs to be brief, clear, and worded in positive terms. In other words don't convey the impression that you are there to "fix" a deficiency in the participants. People are not broken machines to be repaired. Rather, your role is to build on their knowledge and support them in making new connections with the information presented.

It is absolutely essential that the opening be upbeat and that you show energy and enthusiasm. Share your personal connection with the topic and a word or two about your background. This is not a time for a lengthy bio, however. Long, detailed personal histories make the introduction of your workshop lopsided. Instead, make your opening statement about your background and credentials very brief. Later during the course of your session, you can weave in other relevant tidbits about your background. Be sure to state the correct pronunciation of your name if it is difficult to say.

There are a number of different opening strategies you can use, but try to tap participants' curiosity and generate their interest with your very first sentence. I think the best openings appeal to emotions, not reason. It is your motivational hook to the rest of the day. Here are a few possibilities:

- **Ask a question.** You can ask a rhetorical question ("Have you ever been so frustrated with the staffing crisis you've thought of closing your center?") or a question that draws participants in immediately ("What is the single most challenging obstacle you face in recruiting quality staff?"). Having participants do or say something near the beginning of the workshop establishes the understanding that they will be actively involved during the session.

- **Share a personal story.** Starting out with a real-life experience or scenario that participants can relate to helps them connect emotionally with the topic. When I do training on interpersonal communication, I share an amusing tale of an airplane flight I once took and how the garbled miscommunications of the flight attendants ended up creating a windfall for the passengers in free coupons and travel vouchers. The story only takes about three minutes to tell, but it captures perfectly the importance of clarity in interpersonal communications.

- **Display an eye-catching visual.** Projecting a visual that is humorous or imaginative can focus participants' attention on the topic. I love to start workshops by showing a cartoon or zany illustration. I find they are very effective for interjecting a bit of levity into the first moments of the session and setting the tone for a lively, fun day. One of my favorites is an illustration I use to open a stress management workshop. The illustration shows a zebra whose stripes are unraveling. I've added the caption, "I think I'm under stress." As I display the illustration, I ask participants if they've ever felt like this zebra.

- **Make a provocative statement or share a shocking statistic.** Surprising participants with an unexpected statement or headline-grabbing statistic can serve as a call to action, getting people fired up for what comes next. "During the course of this workshop, three children are going to die in America as a result of gunfire. By the time you wake up tomorrow morning, nine more will have died. Today we're going to explore some of the steps you can take as administrators to curb violence against children." Just a reminder — if you use statistics, make sure you are able to cite the source.

- **Use a prop to demonstrate a point.** Props can be very effective for gaining attention at the beginning of a workshop. A friend of mine who led a computer training session for a group of early childhood administrators began his session by asking participants, "Have you ever felt so frustrated with your computer that you wanted to throw it on the ground?" He proceeded to pick up a computer and throw on the ground. He then said, "After today, you'll never have to feel that frustrated again!" (The computer, it turns out, was one he had retrieved from a junkyard). Needless to say, he got the group's attention.

By the end of your opening, participants should know why the topic is relevant to them. They should have a sense that you are prepared, organized, and primed for a day of learning. Having aroused their interest, you are now ready to turn to the remainder of the business to be taken care of during the introduction — clarifying expectations.

Clarifying Expectations and Aligning Goals

After beginning the session with an energizing opening that peaks interest and sets the tone for the workshop, you need to take a few minutes to clarify expectations about what the workshop will and will not cover. Everyone attending the session is asking themselves, "What's in it for me?" This is your opportunity to address that question. Again, the time you devote to clarifying expectations depends on the total length of your workshop, but it should probably not exceed 10 to15 minutes.

When participants walk through the door, they come with preconceived notions of what the experience will hold for them. Those notions may be positive or negative, grand or small. If they have voluntarily decided to come to the workshop and are enthusiastic about the topic, the chances are obviously greater that there will be goal alignment than if they were coerced or required to attend.

Teaching does not equal learning

A cardinal principle of training is that *teaching* does not equal *learning*. For learning to occur, your audience must see the relevance of the new ideas to their lives. Interest in new ideas and willingness to adopt them is activated when individuals believe the knowledge and skills might address their needs. Alignment of goals means taking time at the beginning to share your goals and expected outcomes for the session and having participants share their hopes and expectations of what the learning experience will achieve. It is a two-way process.

Alignment of goals achieves two purposes. First, it underscores your training philosophy that participants are in charge of their own learning; that regardless of your talent and expertise as a trainer, you cannot force them to learn. Second, airing differences in expectations can help you understand the behavior of participants and adjust your training style and workshop plans accordingly.

When differences in expectations occur

It is not uncommon for differences to surface. Participants often come with grandiose expectations for the day, perhaps believing that your workshop will teach them skills needed to make major transformations in their knowledge base or behavior. Just because there is a mismatch in expectations, however, does not mean that all is lost. A case in point. Several years ago I was asked to give a workshop for a social service agency that housed a large child care program. In my discussions with the education coordinator who planned the training, we agreed my six-hour workshop on learning environments would provide an understanding of how space affects behavior, the principles of good design, and lots of suggestions for effective room arrangements that they could apply after the workshop.

On the day of the training, when I shared my goals with the 40 participants, I could see a few puzzled expressions. When I asked if my objectives matched their expectations, I learned that they had been told that I would be touring their classrooms and providing onsite feedback during the day.

Clearly there was a mismatch between my expectations for the day and their expectations. I felt I had been thrown a curve ball. Instead of assigning blame for the miscommunication, however, together we renegotiated the objectives for the day. I modified my original schedule and was able to accommodate their desire for on-site feedback. Discussing expectations at the beginning of my workshop helped me realign goals and respond to their needs. If I had not done that, the group probably would have sat politely through my workshop and zapped me on the final evaluations.

There is another reason for allotting time at the beginning of your session to clarify expectations. At large conferences, the program description for workshop sessions does not always accurately describe the session's content. Indeed, in some instances, conferees select a workshop to attend based only on the title or time. Once the session has started, they may discover the session is not what they thought it was going to be but feel trapped and unable to leave. To prevent this problem, it is essential at conference workshops to briefly indicate what the session will cover and then give permission for anyone who thought the content would be different to excuse themselves and leave.

Linking workshop goals to personal goals

Once there has been an alignment of goals, it is helpful to take a few minutes for participants to think about their personal learning objectives for the workshop. This means translating the broad aims of the day into personal objectives relevant to their individual needs and interests. You can do this by having participants take three minutes to compose their personal goals on paper or turn to a learning partner and share their thoughts.

You can also structure this short exercise around the *Know, Want, Learn* (KWL) framework. Ask participants what they *know* about the topic, what they *want* to know about it, and what they hope to *learn* from this workshop.

Bridging the distance from general expectations to personal expectations is important because it underscores your workshop philosophy that a workshop's success is the equal responsibility of the leader and the group. Aligning goals makes it clear from the beginning that participants are expected to solve problems and actively process information rather than sit passively and receive the gift of your wisdom.

Reviewing the Workshop Schedule and Agenda

When you have clarified expectations for the day, you can share some of the organizational details of the session, previewing the workshop schedule and orienting participants to the content to be covered. For half-day workshops this segment should take only five minutes. The goal is simply to forecast the day by giving participants an understanding of how time will be structured.

There are two types of workshop agendas to consider: a time-block agenda where content is related to specific blocks of time, and a topic agenda where the content is presented in outline form without specific times noted. If you use a topic agenda, you still need to communicate to participants when you anticipate taking your breaks and having lunch. You can present this on a piece of flip chart paper tacked on the wall or just communicate the information orally.

The key in using both types of agendas is not to present too much information about the specific instructional strategies you will be using. Give people an advanced organizer for their learning, but maintain maximum flexibility to modify your schedule if necessary to meet the participants' specific needs. The following examples were drawn from the workshop design matrix on page 43.

Time-Block Agenda

Circle of Influence
**Implementing Shared Decision Making
and Participative Management**

8:30	Welcome, Goals and Objectives, Participant Introductions
9:00	Different Roles Lead to Different Perceptions
9:30	What is Participative Management?
10:00	Break
10:30	Perceptions of Power and Influence
11:15	A Framework for Shared Decision Making
12:00	Lunch
1:00	Getting Started
2:00	Break
2:15	Decision Making in Action
3:30	Break
3:45	Wrap-up

Topic Agenda

Circle of Influence
**Implementing Shared Decision Making
and Participative Management**

I. Welcome
- Goals and objectives for the day
- Participant introductions

II. Different Roles Lead to Different Perceptions

III. What is Participative Management?
- Three principles of collaboration

IV. Perceptions of Power and Influence
- Assessing decision-making style and work style

V. A Framework for Shared Decision Making
- Four questions to guide the process

VI. Getting Started
- Creating a supportive environment

VII. Decision Making in Action
- Consensus building

VIII. Wrap-up

In reviewing the agenda, restate the value of the workshop content. Remind participants why the information is important to them and how they can apply the content to their work settings.

Setting Ground Rules

Workshops run more smoothly when participants understand the expected norms for appropriate conduct and participation. Sometime during the opening of your workshop, it is important to establish the ground rules for behavior. How you handle this will depend on the length of the workshop. For workshops less than two hours in length, you can simply state your expectations to the group and ask for buy-in. For workshops spanning several days, work collaboratively with the participants to develop a set of ground rules to serve as your working agreement.

On the following page is an example of a working agreement generated by participants at a three-day workshop. Table groupings were asked to come up with five suggestions to contribute to a whole-group list. These items were shared and redundancies eliminated. Then, through a consensus voting procedure, participants were asked to indicate the strength of their support for each item on the list. If any member of the group objected to an item, it was either reworded or dropped from the list. The entire exercise took 20 minutes.

Sometime during the opening you need to cover the logistics of the event. Let participants know the location of restrooms, pay telephones, and fire exits and where lunch will be served. If you feel comfortable letting people interrupt you to ask questions, be sure to let them know up front. Also, if you don't mind if people get up to refill their coffee cups or to go to the restroom as needed, make an announcement to that effect.

Working Agreement

We agree to ...

- Speak freely but not dominate the discussion
- Keep focused on the topic at hand
- Avoid private conversations while someone else is talking
- Listen attentively
- Appreciate different points of view
- Return from breaks and lunch on time
- Think outside the box — be creative and imaginative
- Discuss all the issues — don't skirt anything
- Presume positive intentions
- Not chew gum during training
- Maintain confidentiality of information
- Keep our cellular phones and pagers turned off

Icebreakers and Warm-ups

The typical ritual of having participants go around the room and tell their name, job title, and organization may have some value, but most often it is a meaningless activity because responses are inaudible and people aren't really tuned in to the person speaking. They're engaged in merry-go-round listening — getting ready for their own turn to speak. Participant introductions of this sort are not only boring, they are also inappropriate for groups larger than 20 because they take too much time and the information shared is impossible to remember.

Think about using an icebreaker or a warm-up activity at the beginning of your workshop to energize the group and build momentum right from the start. The purpose of icebreakers and warm-up activities is to increase participants' energy and interest, help them ease into and feel comfortable with the learning environment, and give them a glimpse into the key ideas that will be developed as the workshop unfolds.

Icebreakers are social in nature; they help participants meet one another and find personal connections that facilitate group interaction. By getting everyone involved, icebreaker activities help build group identity and cohesion. An icebreaker gives people permission to talk to other people they might not otherwise talk to and about things they usually don't discuss. If everyone attending the workshop already knows one another, then an icebreaker is not necessary. You can move right into a warm-up activity.

Warm-up activities relate to the topic of the workshop. They are designed with a specific goal in mind. Their purpose is to get participants thinking about the topic in a fun and engaging way. A warm-up activity can be conducted during your opening or after a review of the day's agenda. It can serve as a way for participants to express their reasons for coming and their goals and expectations about learning from the workshop.

Because icebreaker and warm-up activities set the tone and pace for the workshop, choose them carefully. Your selection of the right activity depends on the topic of the workshop, the composition of the group, the setup of the room, the length of the session, whether participants know one another, and your style and personality as a trainer.

A workshop of less than two hours allows only 10 minutes for the activity, whereas a workshop that spans several days can easily absorb a full half-hour for an icebreaker or a warm-up activity. In conducting both icebreakers and warm-ups, you need to control the amount of time tightly. It is easy for time to slip away when individuals have a lot they want to say about themselves.

I think the most interesting icebreakers and warm-up activities are those that provide a glimpse into the attitudes, values, personalities, or concerns of the participants. There is no limit to the creative ways you can structure such activities. Use your imagination to think of innovative ways to use games puzzles, quizzes, children's toys, or props to get people energized and ready for a day of training. The key is to keep your activity short and simple. Also, be sure the activity you plan will not embarrass people or put them on the spot.

Here is a selection of activities from which to choose.

What are we having for lunch?

This activity serves a dual purpose; it gets people talking with one another while at the same time providing participants with important logistical information about your workshop. Prepare a stack of 5 x 7 inch index cards, with a pertinent question relating to the workshop on the left-hand side of the card and the answer to the question on the right-hand side of the card. Questions can include such things as

- ✔ What are we having for lunch?
- ✔ Where is the women's restroom?
- ✔ Where is the nearest public telephone?
- ✔ What time will we be taking our morning break?

Cut the cards so that they look like two puzzle pieces that fit together. Distribute the cards randomly to participants so each person has either a question or an answer. Provide time for people to mingle, and find their question and answer match. Afterward, post the cards on the wall for all to see.

Nerf Ball toss

This activity is good for groups smaller than 20. Assemble participants in a circle. Toss a Nerf Ball to one person and ask that person to disclose something unusual about herself or himself. It could be the person's nickname, favorite junk food, favorite childhood toy, or any other question you can think of. Then have that individual toss the ball to another person, repeating the process. With a group of 15, you may get through three or four questions. You can use a Koosh ball, beanbag, or tennis ball as a variation of this activity.

Round-robin recall

This is another activity for a group no larger than 20. Begin with the first person stating his or her name ("I'm Jill"). The next individual then repeats the first person's name and adds her or his own name ("That's Jill and I'm Mark"). Continue around the circle, having individuals repeat the names that have been mentioned and adding their own. To add some fun, award a prize to the last person in the circle if he or she can repeat everyone's name without making a mistake.

Pair and share interview

This is a good activity for a large group. Pair participants with someone they do not know and give them five minutes to interview one another. They can ask the usual questions, like the person's job title, or agency, but encourage them to also find out some unusual information about the other person (an unusual family pet, a wild and wonderful vacation the previous summer). Then ask each pair to pair up with another twosome. Each person can introduce his or her partner to the other pair.

My name is special

Go around the room and ask individuals to share the special significance of their name or nickname. You may need to monitor the time carefully because some people will want to tell you about their entire family lineage to put their name in a historical context.

I feel like a . . .

Ask, "What kind of animal do you feel like today and why?" Participants can go around the room and share their answers. As a variation, ask them to think of the vegetable or color that they feel like.

If I could . . .

Ask participants the following questions: "If you could have lunch with any celebrity, who would it be and why?" "If you could travel back in time to any era, what era would it be and why?" Have them share their reflections with the group.

"Just like me"

Laura Lipton uses this activity in her workshops to build group identity and awareness. It is particularly good with large groups because it can be done quickly. Tell participants that you are going to make "I" statements, and if a statement is true for them, they should stand up and say "Just like me!!" They can then look around to see who else in the group has this thing in common. For example, you can say, "I work in a Head Start program," "I am the director of an NAEYC accredited program," "I got up before 6 a.m. today," "I grew up on a farm." Vary the items that you use to be sure that all participants have an opportunity to stand up at some point.

What do we have in common?

When you have collected information about the participants before your workshop session, you can play a personalized icebreaker that asks them to think about the characteristics they have in common. Code each person's name tag with four or five color dots based on common characteristics. Categories could include such things as gender, role, dog owner, vegetarian, married. During the course of the day, ask participants to try to discern what the people wearing the same color dots have in common. Share results at the end of the day.

Card swap

Make a pack of 3 x 5 inch index cards with different preferences on them: I love burritos, I love country music, I love to drive fast, I like to paint my toenails, I hate to do the laundry, I love lobster, I like Kenny G, I love to Salsa dance, I hate to balance my checkbook, I like to play poker, I hate answering machines. Hand out four or five cards randomly to people and ask them to mingle and trade so that the cards they end up with reflect who they are.

Past, present, future

This icebreaker comes from Julius Eitington's terrific book, *The Winning Trainer*. It is good for workshops that stretch over several days where you want participants to get to know one another well. Distribute a piece of flip chart paper to participants and have them divide the paper into thirds any way they want to with a felt-tipped marker. They should label the three sections of their paper "Past," "Present," and "Future." Ask participants to draw pictures, symbols, words, or phrases in each section that capture the highlights of their past, what they are doing at present, and what they hope to be or achieve in the future. When I use this activity, I also take a Polaroid picture of each person so they can post their photo along with their flip chart bio on the wall for all to see.

I like to use this activity when I have contracted to do a two-part training for an organization. After the first workshop I collect the wall hangings. I review them several weeks or months later before I return for the second part of my training.

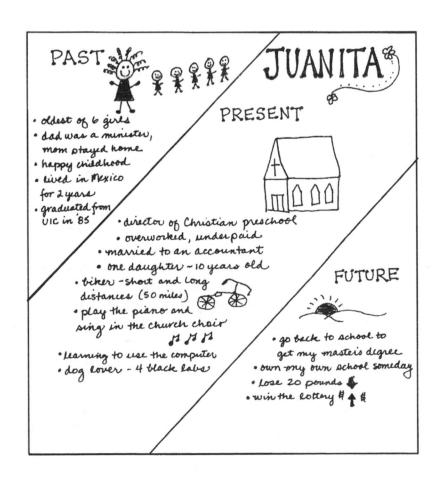

Share and tell

If you have contact with participants before your workshop, ask them to bring with them an item that has some personal significance — a memento, photograph, childhood toy, favorite book, best recipe — that they can share with the group. The timing on this activity needs to be monitored carefully. I have found that participants tend to stretch their minute-long introductions into five-minute monologues when they are describing an object that has emotional significance to them.

Lottery fever

Ask participants to pretend they have just won the state lottery. Ask them to answer the following questions: "What car are you going to buy?" "What country are you going to visit?" and "What charity are you going to support?"

Birth order

Ask individuals to assemble into different groups based on their birth order (oldest born, middle child, youngest child). Depending on the number of participants in the workshop, you may want to add some additional categories (only child, all girls, more than six siblings, twin, triplet). Ask the members in each group to discuss what they have in common. How did their birth order help shape their view of the world?

Getting to know you

Give participants a list of personal characteristics (I drive a minivan, I own a snow blower, I sing in the shower, I own a Dalmatian, I am allergic to bee stings, I know how to change the oil filter on my car, I've been to Istanbul, I speak Hebrew). Their task is to find a person in the group for whom the statement is true. That individual signs next to the item. To liven the atmosphere, you can play "Getting to Know You" from *The King and I* soundtrack while participants are collecting signatures.

You can turn this icebreaker into a game and award a prize for the individual who has collected the most signatures in an allotted time period. If you have conducted a needs assessment or talked to the participants before the training, you can personalize this activity by including information that represents the uniqueness of the participants attending the workshop. Appendix C contains a list of characteristics I put together for a recent training.

What's in my purse/wallet?

This is a good icebreaker for a large group when individuals are seated at tables. Ask participants to go through the contents of their purse or wallet and select one item (picture of grandchildren, key chain from Disney World, lucky charm) that is special or is representative of their personality. Ask them to share the item and its special significance with the others seated at their table.

I bet you didn't know . . .

Challenge participants to think of something that is unique and distinguishes them from everyone else in the room. It could be something they have accomplished (black belt in karate), a personal experience they have had (marched in the Rose Bowl parade), or something they own (a pet boa constrictor). Take turns sharing, "I bet you didn't know . . ."

Lifeline

Ask each person to draw a lifeline depicting five major events or critical incidents in his or her life to share with the group. This is a good activity for a group that will be working together for a long period of time because the lifeline events will serve as a springboard for future one-on-one discussions between participants. Be sure to establish a time limit for this icebreaker, or participants will be tempted to give long-winded details of each critical incident. I once had a woman go on for 10 minutes describing the birth of their first-born child (he was born in the backseat of her car) — that was only one of her significant events!

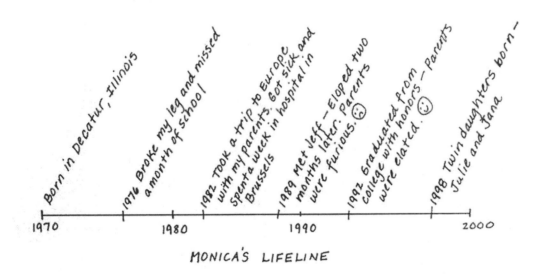

MONICA'S LIFELINE

Pick a prop

My colleague Donna Rafanello uses this icebreaker in her leadership training workshops. It is good for groups of up to 25 participants. Display a variety of props on a table near the door of your training room. Post a sign on the table that says, "Pick a Prop." Props can be almost anything — hammer, Band-Aid, gold coin, kaleidoscope, magnifying glass, key, large rubber band, fireman's hat, string of pearls, eggbeater, whistle. Ask participants to think of how their prop relates to their job. ("My job is like a rubber band. I am stretched to the limits.") You'll be surprised at the imaginative metaphorical connections participants come up with.

If my life were a . . .

Ask participants to share the answers to the following questions: "If my life was a book, the title would be . . ." "If my life was a movie, the title would be . . ." "If I were a song, the title would be . . ." For an icebreaker like this that takes some creative thinking, it is always wise to give participants a little "think time" before you actually conduct the icebreaker. You'll get more creative responses that way.

Same and different

This is a variation of an activity that my colleague Liz Tertell does in her diversity training workshops. It is not an activity that can be done quickly, however, so it is probably best suited for workshops spanning several days where you are able to allot more time to an icebreaker.

Divide participants into trios. Distribute a piece of flip chart paper to each trio. Ask the group to create a Venn diagram on the paper with three interlocking circles. Their task is to think about their personal characteristics that are the same and different and note these in the appropriate spaces on the diagram.

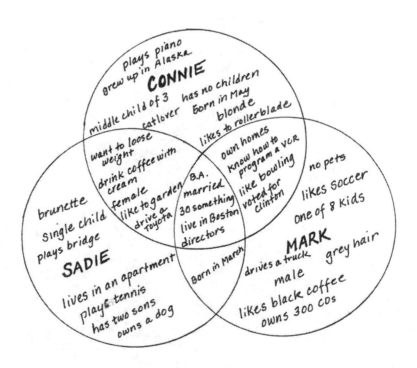

Three numbers

When you distribute name tags to participants, ask them to write three numbers that have some personal significance to them beneath their name on their name tag (4 2 6: "I have 4 daughters, 2 golden retrievers, and 6 months left to pay off my car loan"). As they meet new participants they can share the significance of their numbers.

Personal traits

Distribute a deck of personal trait cards to each person (see Appendix D) describing 75 different personal characteristics. Make a blank card for each person as well. Ask participants to sort through the cards and select the five traits that best described them as a child. If they think of a trait that is not listed among the 75 they can write it on their blank trait card.

Go around the group and ask each person to share their five cards and give an example or two of something they did that typified that trait. Then ask participants to sort through the cards again and select the five cards that best describe them as an adult, providing an example of that trait in action. If the group is larger than 20 people, have participants do this icebreaker at their table groupings of 6 or 7 individuals.

Crossword puzzle

If you know the participants who will be attending your workshop or have elicited some personal information from them in a needs assessment prior to your session, you can construct a crossword puzzle summarizing interesting tidbits of personal trivia. Here is an example of one I constructed for a weeklong training I conducted with a group of center directors.

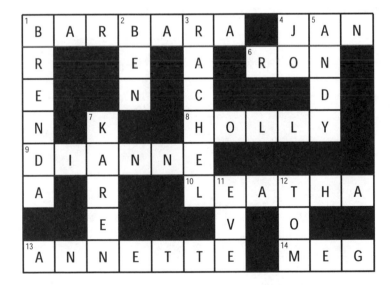

Across

1. Born in Richmond, Virginia
4. Figure skating champion in high school
6. Has a summer cabin in Northern Wisconsin
8. Loves to read romance novels
9. Collects miniature teacups
10. Has two golden retrievers
13. Speaks Japanese
14. Can play the ukulele

Down

1. Is married to an ex-priest
2. Traveled to Singapore last summer
3. Has a twin sister
4. Shook the hand of Nelson Mandela
5. Loves to eat chili peppers
7. Is a Girl Scout troop leader
11. Lost 46 pounds last years
12. Has a blended family of eight children

Who am I?

If you have an opportunity to speak with participants before the workshop, elicit some personal information from them and write a short bio of each person. Include such information as favorite hobbies, special talents, a dream vacation, the most recent book read, favorite dessert, a historical figure they admire, most prized possession, and a phrase they'd like on their tombstone. Distribute the bios without names. During the course of the workshop, have participants see if they can figure out which bios go with what people. To heighten the stakes, award a prize to the person with the most correct answers.

Name tag scramble

From the list of participants who will be attending your session, make up name tags and put them all in a box. When participants arrive, have them select a name tag from the box and locate that person. They can then exchange personal information with him or her.

Baby face

Several weeks before the workshop, ask registrants to send you a picture of themselves in kindergarten or first grade. When participants arrive at the session, hand each a picture of another participant and ask him or her to locate that person and share some childhood memories.

Presentation Style – The Verbal and Nonverbal Ways We Communicate

During the 2000 U.S. presidential primary campaign, Senator Bill Bradley joked about how his image makers tried to get him to change his style so he would be more aggressive in the debates and more assertive in media interviews. After telling him to stand straighter, gesture with more emphasis, and punctuate important words, they added, "And above all, be yourself!"

Fortunately, in a workshop presenter no one expects the perfection of a polished politician. The participants in your workshop will like you if you show you are interested in your topic and you come across as genuine and sincere.

There are things you can do, however, to polish your presentation style so that your message comes across with greater impact. In this chapter I discuss how to blend technical skill and your own personality in a credible, persuasive presentation style. I first address the issue of building rapport — all the things you can do to create a climate of mutual trust. I then look at the importance of honoring the diversity in your group and how differently individuals may interpret the things you say and do. Finally, I consider the importance of physical appearance, voice control, and body language.

Building Rapport

How you perceive your role as a workshop leader quickly determines the nature of your relationship with participants. You can either posture yourself as an expert, thus creating social distance from your participants, or as a partner in learning who is there to facilitate mutual inquiry. Without rapport, a presenter and audience achieve nothing. Rapport is the foundation for a productive and meaningful learning experience — one that makes participants receptive to all the wonderful ideas and information you are so eager to share. But rapport doesn't just happen. It develops slowly, beginning the moment participants walk through the door of your workshop room and you greet them with a warm smile. Here are some of the concrete things you can say and do that will help establish and maintain rapport in your workshop.

Be friendly

This sounds pretty basic, but believe it or not, many workshop presenters come across as being aloof and distant. They are so preoccupied thinking about the thousands of details of what they need to do and say during their session, they simply forget to smile and personally connect with individual participants.

Start your workshop off on a friendly tone. Put a greeting on an overhead transparency or on the cover sheet of a flip chart. Let the participants know that you are glad they're attending your workshop. Review the roster before participants arrive to become familiar with their names and job titles. Make an effort to greet as many individuals as you can *before* your session begins. If you have arrived early and taken care of all the preliminary details of room setup, you should be free to mingle and talk with participants as they arrive.

Make a serious attempt to personally connect with as many people as possible. Obviously the longer your workshop, the easier this will be. Work hard to get to know the names of participants. By using bold lettering on name tags and providing name tents for everyone, you should be able to address participants by name even if they are on the other side of the room. This in itself sets a friendly tone.

I prefer to use people's first names and encourage them to call me by my first name. Being on a first-name basis reduces the status and social distance between the participants and the presenter and creates a more relaxed informal learning atmosphere. The exception to this is when I do training in those foreign countries where tradition dictates that a trainer be referred to by his or her surname and appropriate appellation.

Don't try to impress

While it is certainly important to establish your credibility, don't try to overwhelm participants with your expertise. Bob Pike is fond of saying that the purpose of training is for people to leave impressed with themselves, not with you. To fully connect with your audience, they must accept you as one of them. They want to know that you are a real person, so be open and forthcoming in sharing information about yourself that relates to the workshop topic. Help participants bridge the professional to the personal.

Your credentials and your credibility can be established in ways that are not self-promoting. Resist the temptation to toot your own horn. Shift from an "I know something that you don't" orientation to a "let me share with you what I've been learning and thinking about" orientation. Try not to use jargon that is too sophisticated for participants, but don't talk down to them either. You don't want to come across as patronizing; that will surely turn them off.

The reason why you want to downplay your own role as expert and authority is that your overarching goal for the session is to empower participants to be active agents in their own learning. You are there to help them define important issues, apply tools and techniques, and tap their inner resources to generate solutions to the most pressing problems they face. If you make them dependent on you as the sole source of knowledge and information, you have sabotaged this goal.

Honor the collective wisdom of the group

Empowering individuals to become lifelong learners begins with honoring the individual and collective expertise that participants bring to your session. Rapport is enhanced if people believe that you genuinely respect the knowledge and expertise they bring to the learning experience. I state at the beginning of my workshops that while my role is that of leader and guide, I am also there as a learner. The ideas and practical experiences that are shared during a session enrich my knowledge base and help me become a better presenter and more knowledgeable early childhood professional. I try to communicate that the learning that goes on during a session is reciprocal.

There are a number of strategies that will communicate your seriousness about being a partner in learning. When an individual asks a question during your presentation, resist the temptation to respond with a soliloquy of dazzling insights. Instead toss the question back to the whole group to elicit their best ideas. If a climate of mutual respect has been established, others will leap at the chance to share their insights. You can always add your own two cents worth, but begin by drawing out the expertise of the group.

Here is another strategy I use. When participants first enter the room, I have them write on a piece of flip chart paper the number of years of experience they have had in the field of early childhood (or more specifically in the topic we are covering that day). While I am doing my opening introductions, I have someone tally the numbers. With medium-size groups, the figure often exceeds several hundred years of collective experience. The impact of this sets the stage for my connecting with the group and tapping their expertise. By honoring their expertise, I also serve as a role model for having them honor each other as valuable resources of knowledge and information.

Connect to things that are important to the group

If you travel and do training for groups you have never met before, try to learn as much as you can about the organization they work for. Your conversations with your contact person will be helpful. Find out about the issues participants are confronting and the hot topics they are discussing professionally and socially. If you mingle with participants beforehand, you can pick up tidbits of information and refer to them in the opening 10 minutes of your presentation. This communicates to participants your genuine interest in them.

Take some time to read the local paper, listen to the local news, and talk to staff at the hotel or conference facility to find out what is happening in the community. When you meet participants, if you can weave in a reference to things that are important to them, it helps establish rapport.

A couple of years back I had an opportunity to do training in a town that had been hit by a devastating hurricane the previous year. The fact that I knew details of the tragedy and that one of the preschools had served as a shelter for families displaced by the storm helped me instantly connect with the group of directors attending my training. At several points during my workshop, I used weather and rescue metaphors to emphasize a point I was making or as an organizing idea for a group activity.

Establish eye contact

Eye contact is essential for establishing communication channels and building rapport. As you greet people for the first time, make a conscious effort to look in their eyes for three to five seconds. Communication specialists say that this works best if you actually focus on only one eye; otherwise it appears like you are looking at the bridge of the person's nose. Focusing too long or hard can make someone feel uncomfortable, so after a brief time, pull back slightly and look more generally at the whole face.

When you are presenting, it may look as if you are scanning the tops of people's heads. To avoid this, do a broad sweep across the room and make eye contact with four or five people seated in different parts of the room. Make eye contact for a few seconds and then move on to the next person. Select people who smile or are animated in their facial expressions. Their responsiveness can help you feel more comfortable while you are talking.

Listen with your whole body

Rapport is established when people feel they are listened to and that you care how they *feel* about issues, not just what they *know* about issues. When people are speaking, listen with your whole body. If they ask a question, resist the temptation to jump in and respond too quickly. Pause first and then thoughtfully reflect on what they have said. By attending to the affective elements of their communication — the feelings behind the message — you can respond more appropriately.

We'll come back to the art of listening in Chapter 9, when we address the topic of asking and answering questions.

Don't apologize needlessly

It is amazing how many presenters begin their workshops with apologies. They apologize for not being a good speaker or that the press of time means they'll be unable to cover everything they'd like to on the agenda. They apologize for not bringing more handouts because their photocopy machine broke down or not bringing more resource materials because the airline only permitted two bags.

Participants don't care about your apologies. For the most part, they have no clue as to what you intended to bring or intended to say unless you point it out. Apologizes undermine your attempts to build rapport because they make the audience feel uncomfortable for you. In the end, the apology that you hoped would help you court favor with the audience undermines your credibility as a speaker.

Communicating with Diverse Audiences

Workshop audiences are becoming more and more diverse. Even if the participants in your session all work for the same agency or live in the same community, they are far from homogeneous. They'll represent different ethnic and cultural traditions as well as diverse value structures and belief systems. You may also have participants with disabilities attending your workshops. Communicating respect for the diversity represented is essential to establishing and maintaining rapport.

Make it your personal agenda to heighten your sensitivity to differences of race, culture, and ethnicity so you can avoid unintentionally offending others through a careless use of language or insensitivity to their perspectives. Become aware of cultural traditions as they relate to touch, eye contact, and personal space. One book I have found particularly helpful is *Multicultural Manners: New Rules of Etiquette for a Changing Society* by Norine Dresser. Here are a few things Dresser suggests you keep in mind:

✔ Cultural background affects ideas of what is on time, what is early, and what is late. To avoid unpleasant surprises, explain your expectations about time and ask those from different regions and cultures about theirs.

✔ Although in the United States we stress the importance of eye contact for establishing rapport, there are cultural differences in how people use their eyes to speak and listen. Avoidance of eye contact in some cultures is considered a sign of respect.

✔ Americans smile primarily as an expression of friendliness. People from other places may attach other meanings to smiling.

✔ Gestures do not have universal meaning. For people from many parts of the world, thumbs-up is obscene. Pointing with the index finger is considered rude to people from Asian countries. Also, never use the crooked-index-finger "come here" gesture with Japanese or other Asian people.

✔ Many Asians believe the head houses the soul. To play it safe, avoid touching the heads and upper torsos of all Asians.

✔ In many cultures hugging and kissing on the cheek are acceptable for greeting both the same sex and the opposite sex; however, in some cultures embracing a casual acquaintance of the opposite sex is taboo.

✔ If an Asian participant bows to you, nod your head in response.

✔ In most other parts of the world, a teacher is an authority figure — one to be respected and feared. Therefore, workshop participants in other countries may be shocked by your behavior if you sit on a desk, wear casual clothing, encourage participants to call you by your first name, or engage in humorous banter.

✔ In some foreign countries, you will find participants reticent to speak before the entire group. This is because many cultures consider such behavior as self-promoting, something to avoid.

✔ Many Asians and Saudi Arabians make eating noises to show their appreciation of the food. Consider this a compliment about the food served at your workshop, not as bad manners.

✔ Ethnic groups do not all perceive gender roles in the same way. Some encourage equality of the sexes, and some do not.

✔ In many Asian traditions, the order of first and last names is reversed. To avoid offense, ask which names a person would prefer to use. If the name is difficult to pronounce, admit it and ask the person to help you say it correctly.

Even if the participants in your workshop all represent a single race or culture, guard against making stereotypic assumptions. There are enormous differences in the way people think and process what and how you say things.

When training on foreign turf, take extra time to acquaint yourself with local customs and traditions. Some of the training strategies you use in the United States may not be understood or appreciated in other countries.

A workshop I did for a group of early childhood administrators overseas a while back provides a humorous case in point. To divide the participants into groups, I used a simple grouping strategy that I frequently use back home. I passed out m&ms, one to each of the participants. There were five different colors in two different flavors, plain and peanut. Little did I know that m&ms were not commonplace in the country where I was doing training. When I asked the 70 participants to assemble into 10 different groups by color and type of m&m, there was total confusion. I finally got their attention and asked participants to count off 1 through 10 and find their like groups. I've learned from this experience and a dozen other similar ones to take nothing for granted when training in foreign countries.

In his book *Wake 'Em Up*, Tom Anton tells another story of communication gone awry. This one involved John F. Kennedy. At an impassioned speech at the Berlin Wall, President Kennedy intended to say, "Ich bin Berliner!" ("I am a Berliner!"). What he actually said, however, was, "Ich bin ein berliner!" ("I am a jelly doughnut!") Even Kennedy, who was masterful at communicating, learned that crosscultural nuances sometimes make rapport building difficult.

Norine Dresser tells the story of President Bill Clinton traveling to South Korea to visit President Kim Young Sam. While speaking publicly, Clinton repeatedly referred to the Korean president's wife as Mrs. Kim. The South Korean officials were embarrassed because in Korea, wives retain their maiden names. President Kim Young Sam's wife was named Sohn Myong Suk. Her correct name, therefore, was Mrs. Sohn because in Korea, the family name comes before the given name.

The issue of diversity is particularly important when it comes to the use of humor. It is so easy to offend. I observed a session in England a couple of years ago and the presenter made a casual joke about people in Britain driving on the wrong side of the road. His audience certainly didn't appreciate his egocentric point of view. With that joke he lost any hope of establishing a climate of trust and mutual respect with his audience.

First Impressions – Personal Appearance

Without a doubt, first impressions are based upon how you look. This certainly doesn't mean you have to look like a movie star to be a successful workshop leader, but it does mean that you need to be well groomed and dress professionally. Your physical appearance needs to be consistent with the message you are sending.

Clearly the expectations for dress for both you and the participants will vary depending on the length of the workshop and the setting. As a general rule, most experts recommend that you dress a bit more formally than you think you need to. It's easy to dress down if you're slightly overdressed, but if you're underdressed, you're out of luck. You will never be faulted for looking too professional, even if the audience is dressed informally. Here are some suggestions as you select your attire.

Don't let your appearance compete with your message

Keep your patterns, accessories, and colors simple. Make sure the fabric doesn't make noise when you move. Avoid jewelry that sparkles, dangles, or makes noise when you move around. What you are saying should be the focus of the participants' attention, not what you are wearing.

Women should watch their hairstyle. There is nothing more annoying than to watch a presenter toss or sweep her hair from her face. A well-placed clip to hold back your tresses will be appreciated by your audience.

If you wear glasses, avoid taking them off and putting them on too often. This can be very distracting for participants. Also, avoid tinted lenses in your eyeglasses because they make it difficult for participants to see your eyes. If you do a lot of training, you may want to consider an anti-reflective coating that eliminates reflection and glare.

One final thought: be sure to check your grooming and clothing carefully in a mirror before beginning your presentation. I attended a workshop where the trainer was unaware that her dry cleaner's tag was still attached to the back of her dress. Also check your breath. It is not a bad idea to have a supply of breath mints handy in the event that the luncheon entrée is doused in an onion and garlic sauce.

Dress for comfort

Your clothes should fit well but not too tight. Women, pay particular attention to your hemline, and remember that what looks and feels good while you are standing can look and feel awkward when you sit. Generally, short or long sleeves give a more professional appearance, but during the summer months a sleeveless blouse or dress may also be appropriate, unless you are training in a country with a dominant Muslin population. The most important aspect of your comfort is your shoes. While two-inch heels may make your legs look great, after four or five hours on your feet, you'll wish you had chosen a more comfortable style.

For men a well-tailored suit and tie is appropriate for a more formal workshop; otherwise a sports coat and well-matched trousers are appropriate. You can easily create a more informal appearance by unbuttoning the jacket or removing it altogether. If you are worried about perspiration, men's fashion experts recommend wearing a white shirt with a 100% cotton T-shirt underneath. Make sure your shoes are comfortable and well shined, and that your socks match and cover any bare leg when you sit down. Finally, take just about everything out of your pockets to reduce bulges and that jingling sound when you move about.

Communicating with Clarity

Because your voice and speech patterns significantly affect how participants relate to you and their receptivity to your message, it is worth the investment of time to analyze how and what you say. Our voices are extensions of our identity. It is natural then to feel self-conscious and uneasy about scrutinizing speech patterns. If you think of your voice as a presentation tool, however, it is easier to be more objective in your analysis of yourself and open to suggestions for improvement.

Every time you open your mouth, your mind is on parade.

Malcolm Kushner

The next time you present a workshop, borrow a high-quality tape recorder and record your presentation. As you play it back, concentrate on your voice quality and voice patterns. Does your voice communicate enthusiasm, confidence, seriousness, and interest? Listen to the volume, pitch, tone, and pace of your words. Is your voice pleasant to listen to? Is it convincing? Analyze your choice of words and your speech patterns. Do you communicate with clarity? Is there congruity in your voice and the message you are conveying? By becoming a student of your own voice and learning to focus on your speech patterns, you can learn to maximize the impact of what you are saying.

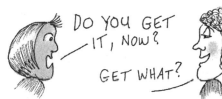

Volume, pitch, and tone

How you say something is as important as what you say. Issues of voice control as they relate to volume, pitch, and tone are usually more of a concern for female presenters than they are for men. Many women's voices simply don't project well. Others do not have that rich resonating quality that makes you want to listen to them for long periods of time. A soft or a high-pitched voice that may be suitable in daily interactions can be a real liability in a workshop setting. If you think you need help improving the tone and quality of your voice, seek out another trainer or a voice coach who will be willing to work with you and give you candid feedback.

In a workshop setting make sure that your voice can be heard by everyone in the room. You'll also want to make sure that your voice volume is consistent and does not fade or trail off once you have been speaking five or ten minutes. If you need a microphone, use it. Ask a participant in the back of the room to give you a subtle hand signal if your voice fades. In most cases, volume issues can be solved with practice. Remember, however, that the resonating quality of your voice varies depending on the acoustics in each room.

It has been said that a monotone voice is the single greatest turnoff for an audience. I suspect this is because vocal variety communicates enthusiasm and energy. Listening to a flat monotone voice is simply boring. Try to infuse vocal variety into your workshop presentation by varying the rhythm, tone, and pitch of words and phrases. Use vocal inflection to emphasize important words and communicate excitement about your topic.

Pace

The pace of your speech also has an impact on participants' ability to stay alert and attend to your message. Talk fast enough to convey enthusiasm but slow enough to be understood. Your pace depends on the size of the group and the acoustical features of the room as well as the participants' familiarity with the topic. If the concepts are new to them, you'll probably need to slow the pace of your delivery.

Learning to pause and use silence effectively is another linguistic tool that can help you craft your own presentation style. Pausing just before and immediately after making an important point that you want participants to consider carefully can be an effective way to underscore key ideas in your presentation. Pausing gives your audience time to think about what has been said and to process the information. Pausing is also an effective tool for gaining participants' attention and redirecting their focus.

Silence can be particularly effective when you sense participants are hesitant to share for some reason. Wait a full thirty seconds before intervening. Often it takes that long for people to collect their thoughts and feel confident enough to make a useful contribution to the discussion. Learning to use silence effectively is a skill that comes with experience; it is one of the tools that distinguishes novice from expert presenters.

Congruity

Congruity means making sure that your voice quality matches your content. When you are communicating something exciting, you should increase both the pitch and pace of your words. When you are communicating information that is serious, deeply emotional, or just plain sad, drop your voice and decrease your pace.

Choosing the *right* voice will help you achieve credibility with your group. In general, when you are giving directions or presenting data, use a voice that goes down at the end of a sentence. This will convey authority and credibility. On the other hand, when you are trying to elicit responses to a question or invite the expression of opinions, you'll want to elevate the pitch of your voice, going up at the end of a sentence. This conveys a more approachable voice.

Articulation and enunciation

If you mispronounce the words you use, you will surely be misunderstood. Try pronouncing difficult words prior to your session and use caution when pronouncing uncommon words. If there are words you think your participants may be unfamiliar with, you may want to post them on a piece of flip chart paper.

Even for experienced workshop presenters, it is helpful to periodically tape record yourself and listen critically to your speech patterns. Here are some things to focus on as you listen to yourself:

- ✔ Do you fill those vocal pauses with um's and ah's?
- ✔ Do you repeat yourself?
- ✔ Do you say "you know" as a nervous filler or "okay" at the end of sentences?
- ✔ Do you use certain phrases like "in fact" so often that they become irritating to the ear?
- ✔ Do you drop word endings such as -ing, -ed, -s, -th, -d, and -ng, making your speech sound sloppy?
- ✔ Does your regional accent or dialect get in the way of communicating your message?

These speech patterns need not be permanent obstacles. By making articulation and enunciation a priority skill area to work on and getting helpful feedback from others, it is possible to modify even the most firmly ingrained speech patterns.

Choice of words

In addition to articulation and enunciation of words, workshop leaders also need to pay careful attention to the selection of words they use, avoiding jargon when possible. Words that are too abstract in their meaning simply muddy the communication waters. As they say, specific is terrific. Concrete words and phrases are more powerful. The effective presenter strives for precision in word choice — words that won't cause confusion or misinterpretation. A statement like "We'll take a break now and start in 15 minutes" is not as clear as "We'll take a 15-minute break now and start again at 2:45."

Big words may look impressive on paper, but in public speaking short, simple, and straightforward helps you win points with your audience. Speak in short sentences and try to use the active voice ("The director conducts a performance appraisal once a year") instead of the passive voice ("A performance appraisal is conducted by the director once a year").

Try to use words and phrases that conjure up pictures in the minds of your participants by using metaphors, similes, imagery, analogy, and symbolism. These communication devices can help captivate and engage your audience. They are powerful tools for generating new perspectives and insights.

Using a metaphor to describe the nature of metaphors, Richard Kopp says, "Metaphors are mirrors reflecting our inner images of self, life, and others." Metaphors are powerful because they engage the mind in making translations from a literal mental language to the analogic, from word thinking to picture thinking, integrating left-brain and right-brain thought.

Think of ways you can use metaphors in your presentations either in the exercises and activities you do or in the lecturettes you present. Metaphors tap the right side of the brain, helping participants remember important ideas and concepts.

One of my favorite workshops I've titled "Images from the Field." It is based on research I've done with directors and teachers about the metaphors they use to describe their organizations, their roles, and their jobs. When a director says her job is like riding a roller coaster, you immediately have a sense of the day-to-day experience that typifies her role responsibilities. When a teacher says she feels like limp spaghetti at the end of the day, you have a keen sense of the physical and emotional exhaustion she must experience daily. Exploring the meaning behind metaphors can help participants generate new ideas and tap insights.

The Power of Stories

In his engaging book *The Presenter's Fieldbook: A Practical Guide*, Bob Garmston makes a strong case for weaving stories into workshop presentations. Garmston believes that people are more influenced by stories than by data. Stories are important for building rapport, making a point, and motivating people to take action. Stories unleash emotions. They can make the themes of your workshop come alive because they personalize the content. Through the use of a story you can sometimes say things to a group that you would not be able to say directly. The right story told at the right time in your presentation can alter attitudes and behavior.

Don't expect to be an expert storyteller the first time you spin a tale. The art of storytelling is honed over time. Some master storytellers say that they practice a story at least 30 times before they feel comfortable delivering it to an audience. Storytelling necessitates careful attention to voice pattern, tone, inflection, facial animation, gestures, and the use of floor space.

Garmston suggests that you plan your presentation without regard to stories. Once your objectives are clear and your content and sequence have been decided, then you can consider what story you know that could support your point.

Sources for stories

Your own personal experiences are the best source of material for your stories. Real stories come from real events in your experience. Write down the details of incidents that have happened to you and keep a file of stories that you can weave into different workshops as needed.

Let me give you an example. For the workshop *Circle of Influence: Implementing Shared Decision Making and Participative Management* (the topic for the design matrix described in Chapter 4), I open with a short story describing the roots of my interest in the topic.

Although it took place more than twenty years ago, I can recall with clarity my first staff meeting as the director of a new child care center. I had read several articles extolling the virtues of participative management and was determined to develop a spirit of shared decision making and collaboration at my center. I carefully orchestrated the details leading up to this meeting. I invited several teachers to contribute ideas for the meeting agenda and reminded everyone about the meeting time. Ever mindful of the importance of ambiance, I arranged the chairs in a circle, put fresh flowers on the table, and brought in home-baked cookies. Finally, I made sure telephone calls would be intercepted to minimize distractions.

During the meeting everyone was polite and respectful, but they clearly were not deeply invested in the discussion. It lacked spirit; it seemed flat. I thought perhaps people were tired after a long day of work and made a mental note to bring chocolate to our next meeting. We adjourned.

Afterward, as I was cleaning up the room, I happened to look out the window. There in the parking lot, the real staff meeting was taking place. The teachers were engaged in animated discussion about all the subjects on our agenda. I scratched my head in puzzlement. Where had I gone wrong? Thus my first lesson in participative management: collaboration does not come easily. I suspect my experience is not unique. Reading about and understanding the principles of participative management are far easier than putting those principles into practice.

I've come a long way in understanding the dynamics of organizational life since that first staff meeting. While I no longer direct a center, I work closely with directors who still struggle with these issues daily. I am convinced that participative management is essential for high-quality program functioning. I am also convinced that implementing it is a complicated and sometimes messy process. It takes patience, persistence, and above all a genuine willingness to seriously consider differing points of view.

In this workshop you'll learn that participative management is both a philosophy and a set of behaviors that define your interactions with people. You'll explore techniques for managing the daily business of your center by involving others in critical decisions affecting their job satisfaction and professional fulfillment. If you implement these strategies and expand your staff's circle of influence, I am confident you will reap the benefits of true collaboration and commitment to shared goals.

I use this story at the beginning of that workshop for several reasons. First, the topic of participative management is an intimidating one, even for seasoned early childhood administrators. I know I won't get past first base unless I connect with the participants on a personal level. Downplaying my academic credentials and letting them know I've been in their shoes is important. My goal is to build rapport though this story. My second goal is to sell them on the importance of shared decision making and forecast what they will learn from the workshop.

Just a word of caution about drawing from your own experience as a source for your stories. Be careful to tell personal stories, but not private ones. Your participants will become uncomfortable if you share information that is private.

Another great source for stories is biographies of famous and not-so-famous people. These can be political figures, movie stars, athletes, spiritual leaders, or just about anyone in the news. Because my area of expertise is leadership and management training, I love to read autobiographies and biographies of prominent leaders.

As I read, I make marginal notes about connections to the themes I include in my training. Marion Wright Edelman's book *Lanterns*, for example, provides some wonderful examples of the power of mentoring. Sidney Poitier's book, *The Measure of a Man*, includes inspirational passages about the importance of believing in oneself. Even a book like Phil Jackson's *Hoop Dreams* is a goldmine of memorable vignettes of how this winning coach cultivated a team spirit out of the over-size egos of the Chicago Bulls. Other books, like *Management by Storying Around by David Armstrong*, *The 21 Irrefutable Laws of Leadership* by John Maxwell, *Moses on Management* by David Baron, and *Chicken Soup for the Soul* by Jack Canfield and Mark Hansen, are filled with these types of stories.

Your friends and colleagues are good sources of story material for vignettes relating to the daily life of early childhood teachers and administrators. Muriel Rand's book *Giving It Some Thought* provides a wealth of wonderful material relating to early childhood issues.

As you develop a repertoire of training topics, be alert to story material from books, movies, and television that relates to your topic. Begin clipping articles and start a filing system to collect stories under topics that relate to your training themes. Remember to share your sources and give credit for stories that you learn from others.

Storytelling style

As you gain practice telling stories, your storytelling style will become your personal signature. You'll learn how to change your voice, position yourself, and add a slight head movement or a hand gesture to emphasize a point or elicit a desired response from your audience. Storytelling style can make or break a story.

Some additional thoughts:

- ✔ Make sure your story is relevant to your subject.
- ✔ Select stories that match the intelligence level, experience, age, and interest of your participants.
- ✔ Space your stories at intervals in your workshop to provide a change of pace.
- ✔ Use the fewest number of words to convey your message in an interesting way.
- ✔ The more credible and truthful your story sounds, the more your audience will get caught up in it.
- ✔ Use people, places, and things with which your participants are familiar.
- ✔ Draw your audience into your stories by saying, "Have you ever had an experience where . . ." "Let me take you with me to . . ."
- ✔ Don't use words or phrases like "funny," "that reminds me of a story," or "I heard a good one the other day."
- ✔ Don't tell a story where you are the hero.

Your Body in Space

Experts suggest that fully 50 to 70% of the force of a message can be attributed to the nonverbal manner in which it is presented. Body language — gestures, posture, stride, facial expressions, movement — transmits powerful messages to an audience about whether to trust and listen to the speaker.

Just as audiotape is a powerful tool for analyzing speech patterns, videotape is the technology of choice when it comes to analyzing your body in space.

The next time you present a workshop, ask someone to videotape your presentation. When you replay the tape, turn off the volume; focus exclusively on your nonverbal body language. Ask yourself these questions:

✔ Do your gestures and facial expressions support your message, adding emphasis and impact?
✔ Does your body move comfortably from one space to another, providing visual variety for the participants?
✔ Do your posture and body movements convey confidence and poise?

Focusing on your use of your body in space helps you become aware of the power of nonverbal communication and make it a presentation asset in future workshops.

Facial expressions and gestures

One of the reasons many people find practicing in front of a mirror so helpful is that you get a glimpse of what the participants see when they look at you talking. As you practice your presentation, consciously think about how your facial expressions and gestures relate to the content of what you are saying. Gestures can be used to help communicate your message without using additional words — a hand on the hip, a shrug of your shoulders, a wrinkled brow, a big smile, a raise of the eyebrows, or a well-timed glance at the ceiling can liven your talk and keep your participants hooked.

Remember that the facial expressions and gestures you use during a group presentation need to be more animated and deliberate than the normal expressions and gestures you would use in everyday conversation with a friend. Try to use your hands deliberately; don't rush your gestures. Your body movements need to appear natural, not jerky. Make sure your gestures are consistent with the size of the room — the larger the audience, the larger the room, and the larger the gesture. Use welcoming gestures at the beginning of your workshop, emphatic gestures to make a point, and sweeping gestures to pull your participants into your message.

The key is not to overdo any single gesture. I used to use the gesture of raising my hand and tapping it in the air (like swinging a conductor's baton) whenever I wanted to stress a point. When I studied a videotape of my presentation style, however, I realized that this gesture had lost its impact because I used it way too often. In fact, I realized it was probably detracting from my message and bordering on being annoying to the audience.

It took me a while to temper this gesture. When I began consciously avoiding use of the gesture, I realized just how often I had used it. Bad habits are hard to break.

Getting rid of distracting habits and mannerisms enhances the effectiveness of your workshop. Here are some gestures and mannerisms you should avoid:

- ✔ hands behind the back and feet spread in a parade rest stance
- ✔ arms crossed in front of you
- ✔ fig leaf pose — folding your hands over the body below the waist
- ✔ gripping your hand in a fist
- ✔ pointing an index finger
- ✔ grooming your hair
- ✔ adjusting your undergarments
- ✔ looking at your watch
- ✔ playing with a pointer, pencil, or any other item
- ✔ keeping your hands in your pockets
- ✔ jingling coins in your pocket
- ✔ jingling bracelets or jewelry
- ✔ rocking
- ✔ looking over your glasses
- ✔ taking off your shoes

Posture, positioning, and movement

In his book *Wake 'Em Up*, Tom Anton cites two studies from the University of Pennsylvania and the University of Minnesota that found that presenters were taken more seriously if they were standing rather than sitting down. When you stand up, you instantly command authority, attention, and interest. Standing isn't enough, however. Moving around and using space consciously and effectively helps you get and maintain attention. As Anton says, "rigid, feet-glued-to-the-floor presenters elicit loud snoring in short order."

Think about your workshop room as your total stage. When you want to make an important point and keep people focused on you and what you are saying, position yourself front and center. When you have asked a question of a participant or are eliciting responses from the group, you can move to a less prominent position on either side. When you want to be playful and really get people involved, move right into the area where participants are seated. The main thing is to vary your positioning to keep the group energized and provide visual variety.

Try to be consistent with your body positioning so that you deliver the same types of messages when you are in certain areas of the room. For example, you may want to go to a certain spot when you are posing a problem, and then move to another spot when you talk about solutions. If you are a person who weaves stories into your presentations, think about having a designated spot for storytelling. The key is to make your movements deliberate. You don't want to confuse your audience by walking around too much.

When standing, keep your posture erect but relaxed. In other words, stand straight but not stiff. This is easiest if you position yourself so your feet are pointing toward the participants. Distribute your weight evenly over your hips. This posture is also the best for combating back pain and leg fatigue.

Some presenters like to vary their body placement by having a tall stool to sit on when they tell stories or sit back to listen to a group presentation. Being able to sit down occasionally during a long training also helps prevent your back from feeling so fatigued.

The act of coordinating audiovisual equipment and visual aids while you are talking is difficult and challenging, but try to be mindful of the placement of your body. Even when you are showing transparencies on an overhead projector, it is best to face your audience. This posture helps reinforce your presence. It also helps with voice projection. Read your transparencies on the projector, rather than turning to face the screen. Once your transparency is projected, you can step away and move toward the audience or to the side. Avoid walking between the projector and the screen or your silhouetted image will be projected big and bold for everyone to see.

Maintaining Momentum and Ensuring Involvement

If you are an experienced presenter, you know that a certain percent of the time, a certain percent of the participants in your workshop will be following their own thought patterns and not fully attending to your message. Their own child care issues, the holiday party coming up, and all the other items on their mental to-do lists are vying for their attention. The question is how do you make your content more enticing than any of the dozen other things they could be thinking about?

Involvement doesn't just happen in a workshop. It is the result of a carefully orchestrated design that heeds the timing of different activities and the selective use of different instructional strategies to keep people energized and attentive. The key is finding ways to engage people physically, mentally, and emotionally.

Look back at the retention pyramid on page 26. If it is true that people retain only 5% of what they hear, 10% of what they read, and 30% of what they hear and see, as compared to 75 - 90% of what they say and do, it makes sense to involve people as actively and fully in the learning process as possible. This is the key to both buy-in and retention.

Look at the workshop design matrix you've prepared for your session. If your workshop is a six-hour block of time, think about the points during the day when you can anticipate momentum beginning to fade. Transitions between topic areas, returns from breaks, and that predictable slump that occurs immediately after lunch are just a few of the times you will want to pay careful attention to.

Tune in to the nonverbal cues that participants' attention may be waning — blank stares into space, rummaging through purses and tote bags, sidebar conversations. These are obvious clues that you may need to provide a change of pace, interject some levity to perk up spirits, or find a creative way to pull participants back into your spell. Your ability to sense momentum shifts and recharge your group accordingly has a decided impact on your overall effectiveness as a presenter.

Listeners will reach their saturation point long before you run out of things to say.

Roger Neugebauer

This chapter looks at some of the many things you can do to maintain momentum and increase the likelihood that participants will stay actively engaged in learning. It begins with some tips for maximizing involvement. It then provides a selection of instant energizers, games, and interactive strategies you can use to get and keep people focused. Next it gives suggestions for asking and answering questions and reinforcing learning connections. The chapter concludes with some advice from the pros about how to handle difficult participants.

Tips for Maximizing Involvement — A Baker's Dozen

To maximize opportunities for involvement in your workshop, you need to consciously think about ways you can adjust your teaching style to encourage and reward participation. Here are a few tips to get you started:

- **Involve participants in different roles.** Individuals can serve as scribes recording information on the flip chart for you and as assistants helping to distribute handouts and materials. You can also appoint an individual to serve as timekeeper, whose job it is to ring a cow bell or hit a buzzer when it's time to take a break.

- **Award prizes.** Give participants small, inexpensive novelty items such as posters, mugs, pencils, and stickers as prizes for different activities and games. Depending on the month of your workshop, you can tie these small prizes to the season or an upcoming holiday (for example, bubble solution in the summertime, miniature pumpkins in the fall). When appropriate, present certificates at the end of training.

- **Ask for a volunteer to serve as the group memory.** This person can help latecomers catch up with information they missed. This individual can collect handouts and take notes for late-arriving participants.

- **Schedule breaks for odd times.** For example, "We'll break at 11:05 and return at 11:20." This helps ensure that a 15-minute break doesn't stretch into 30 minutes. Play music during breaks, and raise or lower the volume to signify the end of the break.

- **Build suspense.** One way to help folks return from breaks on time is to leave them with a verbal cliff hanger just before you take a break — an intriguing question, a provocative statement, or the first part of a joke. Tell them you will provide the answer, response, or punch line immediately following the break. This provides an incentive to return from the break promptly.

- **Anticipate a post-lunch slump.** Avoid showing slides or a videotape immediately after lunch. The combination of a full stomach and a dark room is an invitation to take a siesta. Instead, plan an interactive exercise immediately following lunch that gets people moving around and talking.

- **Schedule shorter and more frequent breaks in the afternoon.** If your workshop is an all-day event, schedule your first afternoon break no later than one hour into your afternoon session.

- **Use enticements to get people to return from breaks on time.** Play a quick trivia game or word puzzle relating to your topic just as a break ends to encourage people to get seated and reconnected.

- **Let people know when you are making an important point.** Cue participants when it is important to tune out their inner thoughts and tune in to what you are saying. You can say, "Here is an important point I want you to remember" or pretend to speak through an imaginary megaphone by cupping your hands around your mouth and say, "Attention, attention, the key point here to remember is. . ." Another way to stress the importance of key points is to physically move to a designated, imaginary hot spot on the floor to indicate a hot or important idea you want them to remember.

- **Periodically take the pulse of the group.** At different points during your session, ask participants for quick feedback about how the session is progressing. One method is to ask people to stand and face you. Then ask them to register with their bodies their responses to the following questions:

  ✔ "How's the temperature in the room?" Too hot (turn and face left), too cold (turn and face right), just right (face forward).
  ✔ "How's my pace?" Too fast (turn and face left), too slow (turn and face right), just right (face forward).
  ✔ "How's the content?" Too simplistic (turn and face left), too advanced (turn and face right), just right (face forward).

- **Encourage and acknowledge participation when it occurs.** Reiterate that everyone has expertise to share, and provide lots of opportunities for participants to be "on stage."

- **Share participants' good ideas with the entire group.** During a break if a participant makes a valuable comment, shares an interesting idea, or poses a good question that relates to the workshop topic, share it with the entire group when they reconvene.

- **Use microphones.** Participants love to talk into handheld microphones; they like being in the spotlight if only for a minute or two. For groups larger than 50, arrange to have one or more handheld microphones available. Pass the microphone to participants when they ask questions, make statements, or comment in response to someone else's question. While it takes a few seconds to pass the microphone to each new speaker, this strategy ultimately saves time because you won't have to repeat the questions that have been asked.

Instant Energizers

Energizers are short physical exercises and activities that you can intersperse during training to help restore energy and interest. The key to energizers is doing them quickly, in most cases in less than two minutes. If you drag out the activity, it loses its spark.

Group hum

Ask everyone to stand up and face the front of the room. If you have a small group of fewer than 15, individuals can form a circle. Instruct participants to close their eyes, take a deep breath, and then exhale out loud with a well-modulated "ommmm." You can vary this energizer by creating a virtual symphony of "ommmms." Divide the group into four sections and ask members in each group to mimic your pitch, starting with a low "ommmm" and using a slightly higher pitched "ommmm" for each of the four sections.

E-I-E-I-O

Ask participants to stand and sing a vigorous "E" with increasing crescendo. Then ask them to sing out an "I." Continue with "E," "I," "O." Top this off with a round of applause.

Shoulder massage

Ask participants to line up in any order. Then ask them to turn to their right and begin massaging the shoulders of the person in front of them. After one minute have them turn the other direction and massage the person who was just massaging them. Be sure to mention that if anyone has a back problem or is particularly sensitive to touch they can opt out of this activity. Invite them to join you as you walk up and down the line encouraging people to moan appreciative *oohs* and *aahs* to their fellow masseurs or masseuses.

Standing ovation

This energizer is hokey, but groups really seem to love it. If a participant shares an incident or story of a hardship he or she has endured the previous week (the classroom was flooded by broken water pipe, head lice invaded the center, the bus broke down on a field trip), say something like, "It looks like you've had a particularly hard week at your center. C'mon up front with me. We're going to make your rough week end on a happier note." Then ask everyone to rise and give the person a thunderous standing ovation. Keep up the applause for at least a full minute, enough time to cause the person to blush with appreciative embarrassment.

Elbow flexing

Ask participants to stand so they have ample room to their front and sides. Then ask them to point their elbows toward the ceiling and write their names in the air. Continue this exercise by asking individuals to write their names with other body parts — heads, noses, knees, and big toes.

Games

Having fun is a basic human need. As Bruce Williamson says in his book *Playful Activities for Powerful Presentations*, fun-filled games help stimulate healthy interaction between people. Positive experiences of communication, cooperation, trust, healthy touch, teamwork, group bonding, and personal sharing tend to increase and improve as people play games together.

Don't use a game just to entertain, though. The best games are those you adapt for your specific workshop to reinforce the points you make. If you do a game just to fill the time, your participants will resent your taking away valuable workshop time for frivolous activity. Select games carefully. Make sure they fit your presentation style and the objectives of your workshop. Also, make sure they are conducive to the setting. Is there sufficient space? Will the noise or laughter generated by the game be a problem? Are participants wearing appropriate clothing for the game?

In choosing appropriate games for your workshop, consider your overall learning goals as well as the diversity in the group. Remember that different learners react differently to group activities. The imaginative learners you read about in Chapter 3 will love games, whereas the analytic learners may need to be convinced they are substantive enough to warrant their participation. Always provide an element of choice when conducting games. Some individuals may be embarrassed about doing certain types of activities, so it is wise to leave an option for people to observe instead of doing the activity.

If you are conducting a workshop in a foreign country, remember that some cultural groups view learning as a silent, nonparticipatory process. They may experience discomfort when invited to participate in a game, particularly one that involves physical contact.

Name that acronym

I originally put together the list of acronyms in Appendix E for a state legislator who was interested in learning the lingo and jargon of the early childhood profession. I quickly found my glossary could be turned into a great game for early childhood educators. When I conduct a workshop over several days, I use this game on the first day to get small groups working together and sharing their knowledge and expertise.

Things you didn't know you didn't know

There are dozens of books on the market cataloging fascinating bits and pieces of trivia. There are also a number of Internet Web sites that specialize in collecting odd bits of information about things you didn't know you didn't know. One of my favorites is www.corsinet.com/trivia. You can draw from these resources or create a list of your own questions relating specifically to your topic. Appendix F provides a few intriguing trivia facts to help you get started.

Brainteasers

The brainteasers included in Appendix G were drawn from Edward Scannell and John Newstrom's book *More Games Trainers Play*. Brainteasers are great for underscoring the concept of synergy, that creative insight that comes when individuals work collaboratively to solve problems. It is important to set a time limit on this activity to create a heightened sense of excitement for the problem-solving task. As a variation you can structure the activity by asking if there are two or three individuals who would be willing to solve the puzzles independently. Then group the remaining participants in small teams of four or five. The teams almost always solve more of the brainteasers in the allotted time.

What's on a penny?

This activity is adapted from Newstrom and Scannell's more recent book *The Big Book of Business Games*. I use it to underscore the importance of observing details. Begin by asking participants to generate a list on their own, without looking at a penny, of all the distinguishable characteristics of a common penny. Then have them meet in small teams of 4 to 5 participants to compare their individual lists and generate any new items they can think of. When each team is satisfied with its final list of attributes, distribute a penny to each person and compare the team answers with the master list provided in Appendix H. Follow up with a discussion about how we can *see* something as common as a penny almost daily, yet not really *see* it at all. In your debriefing on this activity, discuss ways that participants can increase attention to important details in their environment.

Human spider web

This is another fun activity from Newstrom and Scannell. I use it to underscore concepts of teamwork, perseverance, and commitment to group goals. It is designed for small groups of six to eight people. Have participants form a circle. Instruct each person to extend his or her left hand across the circle and grasp the left hand of another member who is approximately opposite. Then have them extend their right hands across the circle and grasp the right hands of other individuals. Their task is to unravel the spider web of interlocking arms *without letting go of anyone's hands*. The desired outcome is a circle of persons all holding the hands of persons standing next to them. Do this activity only if participants are wearing clothing that will allow them to bend and twist without causing embarrassment. This exercise is guaranteed to generate vigorous laughter, so be sure you have your camera ready.

Hoopla

This game comes from Bruce Williamson's book *Playful Activities for Powerful Presentations*. You'll need two Hula Hoops of different colors. Have participants form a circle of no more than 15 to 20 participants. Ask them to face inward and join hands. Ask two people in the circle to temporarily unclasp their hands and then rejoin their hands through the two colored hoops (the hoops will be resting on top of their joined hands). Tell the group their challenge is to simultaneously pass the two hoops in *opposite* directions around the circle *without unclasping their hands*. One colored hoop goes in one direction, the other goes in the opposite direction. The hoops will cross at some point. The goal is to have each color hoop end up where the other hoop began.

It's best if participants are dressed casually for this game, although I have done it with a group of professional women dressed in business suits and heels. The physical nature of the challenge got them involved and laughing heartily together. When the group has completed the game, take a few minutes to debrief. Talk about their initial reactions to the task when it was introduced. Were they skeptical that it could be accomplished? Did they feel self conscious when it was their turn to wiggle and twist through the hoop? What role did the coaching and cheering of the group have on their performance?

Spooning

This is another activity from Bruce Williamson. It's goal is nothing more than to infuse a bit of total silliness when things are getting too heavy and serious in your workshop. Distribute one metal spoon to each participant along with a napkin. Tell participants to use the napkin to make sure their spoon is completely clean and dry. Then have them rub the napkin across their noses to ensure that they are completely free of moisture and makeup. Then ask participants to take their spoon and breathe on the inside of the curved part of the metal bowl. Next, demonstrate for them how you can gently hang the spoon on the tip of your nose. This activity will transform the atmosphere into instant giggles and lots of laughter. You'll probably have a few precocious participants testing the limits of their physical prowess by trying to walk, talk, and chew gum while they perform this outrageous act.

Word scramble

This game can be played at any time during your training, but it is particularly good in the afternoon as a picker-upper when energy levels are flagging. There is nothing like the surge of adrenaline that comes from a little competition. Select a quote that is appropriate for your training topic — one that is not familiar to your group. It should be at least 12 words long. For example, for the topic of leadership, I use the quote, *Effective leaders motivate people not by the answers they give, but rather by the questions they ask*. Using a broad-tipped marking pen, print the quote on pieces of tag board, one word per piece of tag board. Scramble the order of the words and tack each word card to a wall or easel that is clearly visible to all participants. This should be done when participants are not in the room. Conceal the words with sheets of flip chart paper until you are ready to play the game. Group participants in dyads and give them the following directions: "At the signal I am going to unveil a scrambled sentence — words that when placed in order make a pithy quote. The first team to write down the correct quote on a piece of paper and raise their hands will be the winners." Award a prize to the winning pair.

Interactive Strategies

There are certainly occasions when didactic methods of instruction such as lectures and demonstrations are appropriate for communicating important information. To the extent you can, however, try to involve participants in meaningful ways to share, invent, and discover new insights for themselves. In doing so you increase the likelihood that they stay actively engaged in their learning. As Robert Pike is so fond of saying, "People do not argue with their own data." When participants generate their own data rather than being spoon-fed facts and information, they are more likely to integrate new ideas and concepts into their belief systems and make changes in their behavior.

Interactive strategies are not ends in themselves but rather tools for achieving your workshop goals. The content of your activities must be relevant and meaningful. When done right, interactive strategies can increase cohesiveness, alter group morale, and engage people who might not otherwise be comfortable in traditional educational settings.

Workshop leaders who are new to the role of presenting are often reluctant to use interactive strategies because they believe they won't have enough time to cover all the content of the session. Many fear losing control of the group.

These are natural fears. There is certainly an element of risk in introducing interactive exercises. My suggestion is to gradually introduce interactive strategies in your repertoire of training techniques. As you become familiar with how to manage the group and achieve workshop goals in more participatory ways, you'll want to use them more frequently.

In selecting an appropriate strategy, ask yourself the following questions:

- ✔ Is the strategy appropriate for the type of learning desired?
- ✔ Does the strategy require any special equipment or materials?
- ✔ Does the method require a room setup that is readily available?
- ✔ Will the participants be able to understand the directions?
- ✔ What level of physical movement is required? Will anyone be at a disadvantage?
- ✔ How much time does the interactive strategy take?
- ✔ Is the size of the group conducive to the strategy being considered?

Action gives life to an idea.

Jan Noyes

After conducting an activity, provide time to discuss what occurred during the exercise — the ideas that were generated as well as participants' perceptions of the group process. Finally, talk about how the insights gleaned from the exercise can be applied in "real life" — back on the job in their work with children and families. This activity-discussion-application formula provides a useful way to think about structuring your interactive exercises.

Giving clear directions for group activities is essential. Participants enjoy and feel more successful doing interactive strategies when they are not confused about what they are supposed to do. It is helpful to write out the directions for different activities and post them on flip chart paper or put them on an overhead transparency for everyone to see.

Before beginning an activity, be sure to agree upon a signal for gaining the group's attention when it is time to reconvene. Group activities can be noisy, even rowdy. Your cue can be something as simple as raising your hand in the air, flicking the lights on and off, or playing music. Just don't shout. I have a set of chimes that I tap to "chime in" if I can't get the group's attention by raising my hand. If that doesn't work I pull out my trusty carnival whistle and blow it.

Determining the appropriate amount of time to spend on any one activity can be tricky. Participants need enough time to complete their assigned task and engage in a debriefing discussion, but not so much time that interest starts to wane or they get distracted in side conversations. When groups have begun working, walk around the room expressing interest in what they are doing but not pausing long enough at any one group to make participants feel self-conscious. Just let them know you're available to answer questions if needed to help keep them on track.

The size of your work groups depends on the particular interactive strategy you select. For most problem-solving and brainstorming strategies, small groups of five to seven seem to work well. This number is good for ensuring full participation but not so small that a single person is likely to dominate the discussion.

In small groups of fewer than six people, leadership usually emerges, but in work groups larger than seven participants, it is probably good to designate an individual to serve as group leader/facilitator. You may want to designate another person to serve as recorder/reporter of the group's work. Designating a group leader is particularly important when the directions or the content of the task is complex. Group leaders can be briefed beforehand on how to conduct the exercise and alerted to pitfalls or obstacles that may occur.

There are a number of ways you can select the group leader and recorder. Here are just a few:

the person . . .
- ✔ married the most years
- ✔ with the most pennies
- ✔ who traveled farthest to the session
- ✔ whose birthday is closest
- ✔ with the newest shoes
- ✔ who drives the oldest car
- ✔ who has the longest commute to work
- ✔ who has the youngest child

If you use the leaders to summarize the group's work during the debriefing portion of the activity, be sure to set clear time limits on their oral reports. Ask them to stand facing the participants and give a concise summary of their group's deliberations. For most activities oral reports are limited to one or two minutes. This keeps people from rambling. It also reduces comparisons of leaders' presentation styles. Most important, keeping the reports brief helps ensure that even the third or fourth group has something fresh to contribute to the debriefing session.

Now that we have covered the basics of how to select and structure interactive activities, here are a few strategies you might consider using.

Traditional brainstorming

The goal of brainstorming is to generate a lot of ideas in a short period of time. It is a good strategy to use when you know the participants have sufficient knowledge about the topic to come up with a lot of good ideas relating to a particular issue. For example, in a workshop on attracting and retaining quality staff, I ask administrators to brainstorm creative approaches for recruiting new teachers. I know that every director participating will come up with at least one or two ideas, but the synergistic effect of directors working together will generate some new creative recruitment strategies that no one thought of before.

Because the goal of brainstorming is to generate a lot of ideas, open acceptance of *all* ideas is essential. Instruct participants to withhold judgment (positive or negative) of the ideas presented until all contributions have been made.

When conducting a brainstorming activity, I always ask participants to do some silent brainstorming first, writing down a few ideas on a piece of paper before I put them together in small groups of five to seven people. This is very purposeful. In traditional brainstorming it is not uncommon for people who think quickly out loud to jump in and start sharing their ideas. Others in the group who may have a more reflective style or who are hesitant to speak up often don't get a chance to share their good ideas. As soon as someone speaks, everyone else is influenced to some degree by that person's

None of us is as smart as all of us.

Peter B. Grazier

contributions. What happens is that people have a tendency to start elaborating on the first few suggestions that have been made rather than exploring new and completely different ideas. The number of subsequent ideas is thus limited. I have found that allowing a few minutes for silent brainstorming before assigning people into small groups increases both the quantity and quality of the groups' suggestions.

When a group finishes conducting a brainstorming activity, you may want participants to sort the ideas into categories or prioritize and rank them using some predetermined criteria. For example, you could have them sort all their recruitment strategies into categories they come up with (creative want ads, using local colleges, using parents and current staff, financial incentives) then rank them according to some cost-benefit criteria you present.

Carousel brainstorming

A variation of the traditional brainstorming strategy is carousel brainstorming. Divide participants into small groups of five to seven members. Post sheets of flip chart paper on the wall at least six feet apart. Write a question relating to the workshop topic on each sheet (for example, What are some nonmonetary ways we can reward staff? What are some different financial incentives we can offer to retain staff? What are your favorite interviewing questions?)

Each group stands at a sheet of flip chart paper. Give each group recorder a different color marker to record the group's responses on the flip chart sheet. After three or four minutes of brainstorming, signal groups to move right to the next sheet, read the recorded ideas of the previous groups, and brainstorm new contributions. The color marker moves with its group. The rotation continues until all groups have brainstormed on all sheets of paper, adding their group's suggestions to the ideas of the groups before them. At the end of the activity, provide an opportunity for everyone to take a gallery walk to read what other groups have had to say on each of the topics.

Jigsaw

Jigsaw is another cooperative learning strategy that is particularly effective in workshops that span several days. In this activity participants become experts in a particular area and then share their new knowledge with their colleagues. The advantage of this strategy is that it provides a way for participants to learn new content and to reinforce that learning by teaching the content to others. The jigsaw activity promotes shared responsibility for learning, shifting the status of expert from trainer to learner.

Divide participants into groups of three or four, depending on the number of articles you have to assign. Provide a different article to each person on the team. Ask everyone to read their assigned articles independently overnight.

The following day have people with the same article meet together to talk about the article, highlighting major points. In this expert group, the participants can also talk about how they will teach the material to their home team. After a period of time, have experts return to their home teams and share a synopsis of their article with the three other people on their team.

Home Teams

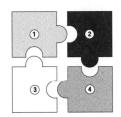 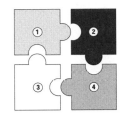 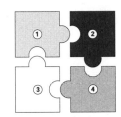 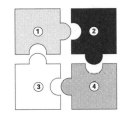

Expert Groups

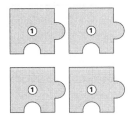  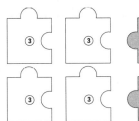 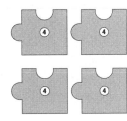

Home Teams

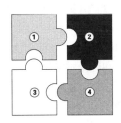 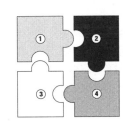 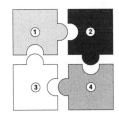 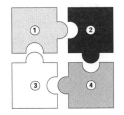

True confessions

This interactive strategy is adapted from Margie Carter and Deb Curtis's book *Training Teachers.* Read a statement, then read four possible answers. Designate one corner of the room for each of the four answers and ask everyone to go to the corner that best represents the answer they consider most accurate or true. Emphasize there is no one right answer, and everyone can determine his or her own meaning for going to a particular corner. For example,

The one aspect I enjoy most about my work is . . .
- ✔ the opportunity to be part of a team
- ✔ the autonomy I have
- ✔ the opportunity for professional growth
- ✔ the opportunity to use my creativity

Once in their chosen corners, ask individuals to share why they selected that particular response. What is interesting about this activity is that people select the same response for different reasons.

The activity is even more lively if the responses are cast in metaphoric terms. Here is one metaphorical variation I used in a workshop with lead teachers:

As a lead teacher I often feel like a . . .
- ✔ kangaroo
- ✔ parrot
- ✔ ostrich
- ✔ bulldog

Synectics

Synectics are another way to tap the power of metaphors for unleashing creativity and generating insights. Laura Lipton and Bruce Wellman, coauthors of *Pathways to Understanding*, use this strategy frequently in their training. The term *synectics*, they report, is formed from two Greek roots: syn — bringing together and ectics — diverse elements. In synectic activities you ask participants to compare two things that they would not ordinarily do. It is a great activity to help people tap their prior learning on a subject and get their creative juices flowing to think about issues in new and novel ways.

Prepare a set of picture cards of everyday objects (kitchen appliances, jewelry, toys, cars, sports equipment) cut from magazines and catalogs. Glue the pictures onto 4 x 6 inch index cards and laminate them to make the cards more durable. Divide participants into groups of five to seven. Randomly distribute four or five picture cards to each group and ask the group to select one card. (At this point participants have no idea what they will be doing with the picture card.) Provide a stem, "How is a staff meeting like a . . .?" Ask the groups to finish the question with the object pictured on their card (a blender, a lawnmower, roller blades), noting all the comparisons they can.

You can also do more open-ended synectic exercises without the cards, where you provide a stem, such as "A team is like a . . ." and ask participants in their small groups to come up with a metaphor (jigsaw puzzle, an orchestra, a forest) to complete the stem. In the debriefing portion of the activity, ask the group why they selected the particular metaphor they did, highlighting the essential elements of their choices and relating those themes to your topic.

Role play

In role play activities participants learn by doing. These scripted or extemporaneous exercises enable individuals to learn new behaviors in the safety of the workshop environment. Having the opportunity to practice new skills, such as being more assertive with a colleague, resolving an interpersonal conflict, or listening to an irate parent, can give participants the confidence they need to apply new behaviors in their day-to-day work setting.

The key to effective use of role play techniques is to make sure the participants approach the exercise as authentically as possible. There is often a tendency for participants to want to exaggerate roles, but the power comes from trying to simulate as authentic a scenario as possible.

You can ask people to play each role exactly as they would in a real-life situation and then provide feedback on the scenario, or you can give them a scripted dialogue of a more idealized exchange to practice and provide feedback on their application of new skills. In either instance the discussion portion of the exercise is critical to the success of this interactive strategy. The actors need an opportunity to reflect upon their assigned roles and share any questions, concerns, or insights gleaned from the experience.

One useful adaptation of the way role play exercises are typically done is to have a participant take on a role reversal. For example, a center director can be assigned to play the role of an upset parent. Role reversal can increase actors' empathy toward differing points of view, helping them to better understand why other people might act they way they do and say the things they do.

As workshop leader you may want to serve as coach, providing feedback, or you can designate this role to one of the participants observing the role play scenario. I recommend doing role play exercises in small groups. This can be as few as three people but no more than seven. I've found that small groups reduce the discomfort "actors" feel about being on stage. I've also found when I keep the groups small, I am able to elicit much more active participation from group members. Only when a large group has established a sense of trust and collegiality do I attempt role play with the whole group watching.

Don't necessarily expect an enthusiastic response when you introduce a role play exercise in your workshop. Workshop attendees usually have mixed feelings about role play activities. They groan when the exercise is introduced because they know they will feel self-conscious being the focus of attention while they are fumbling to master new skills. When the exercise is over, however, they uniformly applaud the approach as a wonderful strategy for helping them integrate new behaviors into their repertoire of interpersonal skills.

Whether you write your own role play scenario or select one from the many resources available, here are a few criteria to keep in mind:

✔ Does the role play situation depict a realistic problem?

✔ Does it include sufficient detail to give the actors a good feel for the facts of a situation, but not so much detail as to detract from the critical elements of the scenario?

✔ Do the characters in the role play have distinctive conflicts?

✔ Is the role play limited to only two to three characters?

✔ Does it provide guidelines for observers?

Think-write-pair-share

The think-write-pair-share activity is one you can use frequently during a workshop. After you pose a question or problem to the whole group, ask participants to jot down their responses to the question or problem on a piece of paper. They need not be formal responses, just some quick notes to aid recall as they move onto the next part of the activity.

Pair participants with learning partners and ask them to each share their response with their partner. This forces them to shift from their internal reflections to articulating their point of view. After a designated period of time, reconvene. In the debriefing discussion, you can ask for volunteers to share their insights with the whole group. By writing and talking with their partners first, participants have mentally and verbally rehearsed what they will say. This strategy gives those who are more reluctant to talk in a large group the confidence to do so.

Card sort

Card sort activities are a good interactive strategy when you want to build on participants' previous knowledge about a topic and build on the synergy that comes when people share their good ideas. The activity entails five steps:

1. Distribute about five to ten 3 x 5 inch index cards to each participant. Pose a question to the group relating to your topic: for example, "What are the elements of a good staff meeting?" "What are ways we can motivate people to peak performance?" Ask people to generate as many ideas as they can, noting one idea on each piece of paper.

2. Next, have participants meet in small groups of four or five. In their small groups they should share their individual ideas, generate new ideas, and combine and reword ideas to come up with a total of 15 to 20 ideas. Each idea should be listed on a separate piece of paper.

3. Ask groups to sort and categorize their ideas, labeling each category. Display these on a table or on the wall.

4. Provide an opportunity for participants to take a gallery walk, looking at the work of other groups.

5. Debrief. Talk about similarities and differences in the ways groups sorted and categorized their ideas. Relate them to the themes of the workshop.

Mobile continuum

One way to get people involved is to ask them to indicate their attitudes and feelings about various issues by positioning themselves at different points along an imaginary continuum. For example, in my workshop on conflict resolution, I like to get a sense of how comfortable individuals feel about asserting their point of view in different types of situations. I draw an imaginary line down the center of the room, and at one end I designate "Very reluctant to do this." The other end of the continuum I designate "No problem doing this." Then I read off a statement and ask participants to physically position themselves on the continuum to represent their response.

Here are a few of the statements I include in that particular workshop:

✔ Tell a friend who gave me a pair of pierced earrings as a gift that I don't have pierced ears.
✔ Tell my supervisor that I find his humor offensive.
✔ Return a jacket to the department store where I bought it after I realize it doesn't match my slacks.
✔ Confront a colleague about her lack of cooperation in cleaning the classroom at the end of the day.
✔ Tell a colleague that she has a personal hygiene problem on hot summer days.
✔ Ask my boss for a raise.
✔ Confront a mother in the grocery story who is belittling her child.

In the debriefing of this exercise, ask participants what they noticed about their own behavior in different situations ("I'm not timid with salespeople, but I am with my colleagues") and about the whole group's behavior ("No one feels comfortable confronting issues of personal hygiene").

Walk and talk

Instead of pairing people and having them just sit and discuss an issue, give them permission to get up, leave the workshop room, and walk and talk about the issue. When they return after a designated period of time, they'll not only have accomplished the task of exchanging information, they'll be more energized from their brief exercise.

Suggestion circle

This strategy is one that Jean Illsley Clarke mentions in her book *Who, Me Lead a Group?* It is particularly effective when you have participants raise thorny issues at a workshop and you want to generate some helpful feedback to guide them in future decision making. The goal of the suggestion circle is to activate clear thinking and tap the wisdom of the group.

Have participants sit in a semicircle. Position the individual who "owns" the problem that needs solving in the open part of the semicircle. Begin the activity by having that person state in a clear, concise way the nature of the problem that needs solving. For example, one teacher is habitually late or one teacher's room looks like a pigsty. One by one, ask each person in the suggestion circle to offer possible solutions. They begin their solution by saying, "You could . . ." or "I would suggest you . . ." The role of the individual who owns the problem is to listen attentively and accept each suggestion with no more than a "thank you." It is best if you appoint someone to write down all the suggestions so the listener can give full attention to listening.

Appropriate/inappropriate

A colleague who conducts a lot of training using NAEYC's publication *Developmentally Appropriate Practice in Early Childhood Programs* developed a set of 5 x 7 inch cards detailing appropriate and inappropriate practices as described in the book. During her workshop she has teachers sort the cards into different groups of appropriate and inappropriate practices. She includes several examples where the distinction is not clear-cut. These examples provide the grist for a lively discussion about cultural or contextual differences in defining what constitutes appropriate and inappropriate practice in early care and education. This activity could easily be adapted to other topics where you want participants to classify issues or practices according to different criteria.

Grouping and Regrouping Participants

To conduct the interactive strategies described in the previous section, you'll need to group and regroup participants during your workshop. There are a number of different ways you can do this. The size of your group and your method for grouping depends on the objectives of the activity, the length of the workshop, and how well participants already know one another. Grouping participants for different activities can be as lively and fun as the activity itself.

Use learning partners (dyads) when your goal is to form one-on-one relationships or when you want individuals to have a sounding board for expressing a point of view or reacting to an issue that has been presented. You can group participants in dyads quickly and efficiently just by asking them

Many ideas grow better when transplanted into another mind than in the one where they sprang up.

Oliver Wendell
Holmes, Jr.

to turn to the person to their right and begin discussing a particular issue. Instantly the room will be filled with the buzz of animated conversation. Dyads are effective because they are nonthreatening to participants; rapport is easy to achieve. Two dyads can be combined to form a foursome. At a later point in the training, this group can even be combined with another group to make a work team of eight. The advantage of this grouping strategy is that some of the participants in the group will already know one another.

Although trios provide greater variety, they should be used sparingly. They are best for role play activities where the scenario calls for two actors and one observer or for jigsaw activities where there are three articles you want participants to read and share. Trios are less effective than other grouping arrangements because the dynamics of the relationships in a threesome can be complicated. Sometimes two of the individuals really hit it off, leaving the third person to feel left out. If you do use trios, make sure participants position their seats in a triangle to facilitate interaction.

The key factor in constructing groups is knowing how many participants you want in each group. For most activities five to seven people is ideal, but there may be some activities where you want as many as nine or ten participants in a group.

Dividing the whole group into subgroups takes some thought. You need to know how many people you have in total and how large you want your small groups to be. Count the number of people involved, and divide by the number of people you want in each group. That will tell you how many small groups you will be forming. For example, if you have 40 participants and you want small groups of five, than you will need eight groups altogether. You can line people up and have them count off by eight. Of course, workshop numbers seldom work out so neatly. You may have 42 people total and end up having six groups of five and two groups of six people each.

If your workshop is only a couple of hours in length, you may have time for only one small group activity. If your workshop is a full-day training, however, try to rotate the groups at least twice during a day. As you regroup, have participants take different seats. This adds variety to their perspective and stimulates networking. For multiday training, consider having a home team that individuals come back to for certain activities. Encourage these groups to create a name and a catchy slogan or song to capture their group personality. Because regrouping participants means having them move out of their comfort zone, be sure to let people know in the opening remarks of your workshop that you will be grouping and regrouping people in a number of

If you always sit where you always sat, you will always see what you always saw, and you'll always get what you always got.

Laura Lipton

different configurations during the session. Stress the advantages of this strategy, letting participants know that they will have the opportunity to sit in different places and meet and work with different people.

A potpourri of sorting techniques

There are countless ways you can randomly divide people into groups. Here are just a few:

- ✔ month of their birthday
- ✔ astrological sign
- ✔ the first letter of first or last names
- ✔ shoe size
- ✔ telephone prefix

There are also many different items you can use to help sort people into groups:

- ✔ playing cards (by suit or number)
- ✔ color paper clips
- ✔ different flavors of gum
- ✔ symbol or sticker on name tags
- ✔ color buttons
- ✔ color m&ms

Famous pairs

On 4 x 6 inch index cards, write the names of famous pairs. Distribute the cards to participants and have them try to find their partner. Examples might include Luci/Desi, Barbie/Ken, Tonto/Lone Ranger, vinegar/oil, Fred Astair/Ginger Rogers, ham/eggs, Bill/Hillary, corn beef/hash, Romeo/Juliet, mashed potatoes/gravy.

Memorable quotations

Select some memorable quotes that relate to your topic. Write these on 5 x 7 inch index cards. Cut the cards in half so they resemble two puzzle pieces. Distribute the pieces randomly to participants and ask them to find the person who completes their quotation.

"Change is the process by which

the future invades our lives."

~ Alvin Toffler

Making connections

Distribute the *Making Connections* handout in Appendix I. Ask participants to spend a few minutes getting the signatures of four individuals in the room, one on each puzzle piece. For each person they ask to sign a particular puzzle piece, participants should sign their own name on that person's *Making Connections* handout on the corresponding puzzle piece. During the course of your workshop, when you want people to get a new partner to discuss and issue, you can say, "Team up with your puzzle piece #2 on your *Making Connections* handout."

Barnyard animals

Distribute to participants slips of paper, each with the name of a different barnyard animal — cow, chicken, duck, pig, horse, dog, rooster. If you have 30 participants and you want groups of six, you'll need five different animals on the slips of paper. At a signal, ask participants to make the noise of their designated animal to locate the other members of their barnyard group. Don't try this grouping activity first thing in the morning, as folks won't be in the mood to moo or cluck if they are barely awake or barely know one another. Wait until you have warmed up the group and they are in the mood for a more playful grouping strategy.

Hum-a-long

Like the barnyard animals grouping strategy, this strategy works best when participants know one another and an air of fun and levity has been established. Distribute small slips of paper with the name of a familiar tune on each piece ("London Bridge," "Yankee Doodle," "Twinkle, Twinkle, Little Star," "Jingle Bells"). At a signal, ask participants to hum their tune and try to find the other members of their humming chorus.

Puzzle pieces

Obtain several children's puzzles that have six to eight pieces. Randomly distribute a puzzle piece to each participant. Ask people to search out the remaining parts of their puzzle to form their small groups.

Using Humor

Few of us have the entertainment skills of a Lily Tomlin or a Robin Williams. Fortunately, as workshop leaders we don't need to. We can draw on the energy, involvement, and spontaneous opportunities that surface during training to create humorous moments of genuine heartfelt laughter and fun.

Humor can enhance the learning that takes place in a workshop setting by allowing people to relax and be more open to new experiences and ideas. Humor arouses interest, encourages camaraderie, and makes you more

To get them listening . . . get them laughing.

Allen Klein

likeable as a trainer. Humor shows that you don't take yourself too seriously as a trainer. It makes your information more memorable and helps lighten up heavy content.

Acquiring a playful state of mind is the only prerequisite to creating a learning environment where genuine good-natured humor can flourish. Infusing levity and humor into your training doesn't mean that you have to be good at telling canned jokes. But it does mean that you need to be alert to those spontaneous moments when laughter is natural and appropriate. The size of your group has a decided effect on the kind of humor that is appropriate to use in your workshop. In small groups you'll find that laughter comes more easily.

Sources of humor

Humor drawn from your own experience is always at hand. Audiences will love your self-effacing humor. It makes you look human and brings the group together as they identify with your trials and triumphs. Avoid at all costs any humor that might offend or alienate participants, and never joke at anyone's expense. Over time, you may have participants who have attended previous workshops you've given, so you need to be on the look out for fresh stories and experiences to share.

Plan the content of your workshop first without concern about being witty or humorous. After you have a good sense of the important themes you want to communicate then think of humorous incidents or vignettes that you've experienced that might connect with those themes.

Here's an example. As I was pulling together the material for the workshop I mentioned earlier about directors' and teachers' metaphors, I recalled an incident that had occurred when I was the director of a child care center. I wrote down the key ideas of the incident first, and then added some descriptive details to help participants form a picture in their minds. I now use this short story as an introduction to that workshop.

> *My interest in directors' role perceptions was prompted by an incident several years ago when I was the director of a preschool. I had just finished giving a new parent a tour of my school. While she completed her enrollment forms, I offered to entertain her son in my office. Jonathan inspected the photographs and plaques on my wall, surveyed the books and knick-knacks on my shelf, and carefully eyed the stack of papers on my desk. He then turned to me and in the unabashed candor so characteristic of a four-year-old said, "You must be the queen of this school." Deciding that a four-year-old wasn't quite ready for a lecture on how queen didn't exactly square with my management philosophy, I simply turned to Jonathan and said, "Yes, I guess a director is a lot like a queen."*

The key to a happy life is the ability to laugh at yourself, for then you are never without a source of amusement.

Katherine Rolfe

Jonathan has since graduated from college, but his innocent remark remains etched in my memory. During these intervening twenty years, I've thought a lot about how individuals view their roles and the power that personal perceptions have in shaping one's professional identity. Different roles in any organization carry with them associated expectations; both self-expectations and the expectations of others.

Because I have rehearsed this humorous vignette many times, I can say it by memory, adding a raised eyebrow and a pause immediately after I say the word *queen*. I know that is the point where I can expect laughter. This is one small example of how your own experiences can be a rich source of material for you to make your ideas come alive for your audience.

My eight-year-old daughter is a wonderful source of humorous material for me. One evening recently at dinner she declared, "Claire and I are good buddies now. Mrs. McNeela sent us to *prayer and meditation* and we don't fight any more." My husband looked at me rather puzzled, wondering if our school district had instituted some version of a New Age curriculum. I let out hoots of laughter because I knew the school had recently implemented a *peer mediation* program for the children to help them work out their differences. This little humorous incident will make a great joke to weave into my training on interpersonal communication and conflict resolution.

Once you tune into it, you'll realize that humor is everywhere. Begin a clip file of humorous cartoons from the newspaper or magazines that relate to your training topics. If you get a humorous anecdote or cartoon from another source, be sure to acknowledge it. There are also numerous Internet Web sites now that are exclusively devoted to humor. Check these out:

- ✔ www.swcbc.com/humor
- ✔ www.corsinet.com/braincandy
- ✔ www.startpage.com
- ✔ www.FunnyScott.com
- ✔ www.mcn.net/~jimloy

There are also many things you can do to create a lighthearted tone in your learning environment. Your workshop announcement and agenda can be decorated with cartoon characters. You can pass out fun snacks, put balloons on participants' chairs, or post humorous signs and graphics directing people to your room. You can post cartoons, funny quotations, poems, and posters on the wall.

When I conduct a workshop in the afternoon, I find that participants often come preoccupied with the work of the morning still buzzing in their heads. To help them make the transition, I start the session with a fun icebreaker I call, "What's on Your Mind?" I ask people to write down on a piece of paper three or four things that are on their mental to-do list. When everyone is finished, I ask them to stand up, crumble up their paper, and hurl it through the air 20 feet or more into a wastepaper basket. I award a prize to the person who makes the basket. If I don't have a wastepaper basket handy, I'll give them permission to have a snowball fight. They all end up with somebody else's to-do list — a sure way to generate some instant laughter.

In a stress management workshop, I do a similar exercise. I ask people to write down a half dozen personal or professional things that are currently stressing them. I tell them these can be big, hairy worries like their income taxes that haven't been filed for the past three years or silly annoyances like the laundry that is piling up. Then I give them precise directions on how to make a paper airplane out of their stress list and give them permission to sail their worries off into the stratosphere. Their challenge is to avoid getting bombarded with someone else's stress bomber. This activity works best in groups larger than 25.

Sometimes you can inject some planned comic relief into your session by projecting a cartoon or picture with no caption. Have teams come up with a humorous caption relating to your workshop topic. Sometimes it is fun to catch your participants off guard. Think of humorous ways you can transpose words so they don't make sense or give some directions that are nonsensical: "Everyone, line up and count off in alphabetical order by shoe size."

Timing

Professional comedians know that timing is everything when it comes to using humor effectively. The time of day you tell a joke or humorous incident impacts your "laughter factor." People need to warm up; they are not conditioned to laugh a great deal in the early morning. Humorous moments in the late afternoon or early evening, as well, often fall flat. Participants are generally most primed to have fun in the late morning or mid-day.

Good presenters plan for spontaneous laughter. They incorporate games, raffles, and props to create a lighthearted climate. For example, when I do a workshop over two or three days, I bring in some plastic clappers and place them on the tables on the last day. I usually do this at a time during the training when participants are making small group presentations. After the first presentation, I can always count on someone in the crowd picking up the clapper and waving it sending a signal to others to join the roar of applause. This strategy would not work on the first day of training because the participants wouldn't feel comfortable initiating that move, but by the second or third day they are primed for fun.

Preplanned ad-libs

In his book *Wake 'Em Up*, Tom Anton talks about preparing preplanned ad-libs that you can inject into your training when the opportunity arises. These ad-libs can keep you mentally ready so you won't fumble for words when problems come up in a presentation. A preplanned ad-lib is a witty comment that appears to be spontaneous. In truth, says Anton, most of the problems that occur during presentations can be expected. The participants will believe you are coming up with a humorous quip right on the spot, but you are just quickly recalling your preplanned response. Here are a few he suggests:

✔ You drop something or something falls . . .
"I hope my point hits as hard as that [name item] just did."
"If it wasn't for gravity, that would never have happened."
"I guess that [name item] disagreed with my last point."

✔ Something is broken . . .
"I would fix this, but I only know how to call for estimates."
"That's what I get for buying this at a flea market."
"I know its time for a BREAK, but this is ridiculous."
"This [name item] just took at break, so why don't we take one too."

✔ The lights go out . . .
"I guess I'll have to donate a portion of my fee to the electric company."
"I hope my presentation hasn't left you in the dark."
"It appears that I need to shed some more light on this subject."

✔ The microphone squeals . . .
"Don't be alarmed. This is only a test."
"Don't worry. I pass out earplugs at all my workshops."
"If you think that's bad, wait until I start singing."
"For those of you who can still hear, welcome."

✔ The projector light burns out . . .
"This is the first time I have been brighter than my equipment."
"I don't understand, I left this thing on day and night for six days to make sure the bulb worked."
"These overhead transparencies are a little darker than I expected."

✔ A slide is upside down . . .
"You may want to stand on your heads for this one."
"I have reversed my position on this issue."
"Maybe if I turn the screen over, you'll be able to see this one better."
"It was really difficult to take this picture."

✔ A marker you are using runs out of ink . . .
"This is the dry part of my presentation."
"I wish I'd bought the extended warranty on this packet of markers."

✔ Someone points out a misspelling . . .
"That was put in there to test you."
"Oh, I apologize. My word processor had a virus."
"If you can't write a word at least two ways, you're not being creative enough."

✔ You trip . . .
"I used to be too humble to stumble."
"Give me an inch and I'll take a fall."

✔ You hear a loud crash . . .
"I always like to start off with a bang."
"I'm flattered. You ordered fireworks for me."

Reinforcing Learning Connections

The essence of being an effective workshop leader is knowing how to take the content you have and present it in such a way that you reinforce learning connections — connections that transform participants' ways of thinking about who they are and what they do. It is not enough to present interesting ideas; get participants involved in interactive exercises, and dazzle them with your creative visuals. The way participants integrate the content and experiences of your workshop into their current frames of thinking is what determines whether your training will have a lasting impact on changing attitudes and behavior.

This chapter explores the many things you can do during your workshop to reinforce learning connections. It begins with suggestions about how to ask questions that move participants' thinking to deeper levels of understanding. From there it looks at how effective trainers use the questions that participants pose to reinforce important concepts and validate personal growth and awareness. It then looks at some strategies you can employ to help people process and recall information. Finally, it addresses the issue of difficult participants and how you can support their internal shift from resistance to openness.

Asking Questions

The kinds of questions you ask and how you ask them can have a profound effect on whether or not participants absorb the concepts and ideas you hope to communicate during your workshop. Well-crafted questions push participants to higher levels of thinking. Questions strategically placed at different points in your presentation can also help you achieve your goal of maintaining momentum and ensuring involvement. Questions can help you

- ✔ check participants' understanding of important concepts
- ✔ emphasize important points
- ✔ correct misunderstandings and misperceptions
- ✔ detect knowledge gaps that may require additional attention
- ✔ surface possible resistance
- ✔ determine if participants' needs are being met
- ✔ elaborate on new learning
- ✔ summarize key concepts

The art of teaching is the art of assisting discovery.

Mark Van Doren

Asking questions of participants should never be done as a filler or add-on to your workshop. Questions need to be thought through as carefully as any other instructional strategy you employ. Your question-asking style can become a signature trait of your workshops and help you achieve rapport with your audiences. Most important, though, the questions you ask can help you get a glimpse into the thinking processes of your participants and assist you in scaffolding from current understanding to new levels of awareness.

Types of questions

As a trainer, it is important to know when to use closed or open questions as well as convergent, divergent, or evaluative questions. The following table provides a description and example of each.

	Types of Questions	
Type	**Description**	**Example**
Closed	• Seeks information, identification, or confirmation • Requires a one-word answer • Usually begins with *is, how many, can, do, does* • Limits discussion	"Do you serve healthy snacks for the children?" "How many of you use a catering service for your lunches?"
Open	• Requires more than a "yes," "no," or short factual answer • Creates more active involvement and stimulates thinking • Promotes continued discussion • Usually begins with *what, how, when, or why*	Subjective: "What do you perceive to be the value of shared decision making?" Objective: "What are the elements that distinguish successful job interviews from those that are not successful?"
Convergent	• Brings together facts and data to form a theory	"Given what you know about your employees, how can directors motivate staff to high levels of performance?"
Divergent	• Stimulates explanation, translation, and interpretation	"What do you think would happen if you implemented a merit pay system?"
Evaluative	• Requires that the individual make a judgment based on an analysis of facts and information	"How would you describe her effectiveness as a lead teacher?"

Adapted from Eitington, J. (1989). *The winning trainer*. Houston, TX: Gulf Publishing and Hart, L., (1991). *Training methods that work: A handbook for trainers*. Palo Alto, CA: Crisp Publications.

Sometimes it is appropriate to ask straightforward questions that merely require participants to describe, recall, or reiterate information. For example,

- ✔ What did you see happening in the video? (description)
- ✔ What did the teacher say that provoked such an angry response from the parent? (recall)

Keep in mind, however, that questions that challenge participants to compare, contrast, analyze, assess, synthesize, and interpret are those that will reinforce learning connections and stimulate higher levels of thinking.

- ✔ Why do you think the situation occurred? (assess)
- ✔ Has a situation like this ever occurred at your own center? How was it similar or different from the scenario you viewed in the video? (compare/contrast)
- ✔ What do you think you could do to reduce the likelihood that such an incident would occur in the future? (interpret)

Phrasing questions

The phrasing of your question has everything to do with how it is received. As a rule of thumb strive for brevity, clarity, and relevance. Long-winded or convoluted questions that cover more than one point only confuse and frustrate participants.

While open-ended questions are preferred, you should also try to avoid asking questions that are too broad. Even a question like, "What was your reaction to the video?" is too broad and lacks focus. This type of question can send your discussion flying in a dozen directions. It would be far better to give the participants a viewing assignment — specific questions to be thinking about as they watch the video. This technique not only serves as an advance organizer in helping them anticipate the content of the video, it also increases the quality of the responses because participants will have had ample time to think about each question as they watch the video.

At all costs, avoid questions that may seem patronizing. If you ask a question that is too simple, your participants will feel insulted. Likewise, if you ask a question that is clearly over the heads of everyone in attendance, it will appear as if you are posturing for expert acclaim. Judging the appropriate level and sophistication of the question comes from really knowing your audience. The most well-received questions tend to be those where you draw on and validate participants' experience: "Georgia, have you ever experienced a similar situation? How did you handle it?"

Guidelines for Phrasing Questions

DO	DON'T
• Ask clear, concise questions covering a single issue.	• Ask rambling, ambiguous questions covering multiple issues.
• Ask reasonable questions based on what participants can be expected to know at that point in the workshop.	• Ask questions that are too difficult for the majority of participants to answer.
• Ask challenging questions that provoke thought.	• Ask questions that are too easy and provide no opportunity for thinking.
• Ask honest, relevant questions that direct participants to logical answers.	• Ask "trick" questions designed to fool participants.

From Hart, L. (1991). Training methods that work: A handbook for trainers. Palo Alto, CA: Crisp Publications, p. 59. Reprinted with permission.

When asking a question, it is essential to use an approachable voice where the inflection and pitch curl up slightly at the end. Also, phrase your question in the plural form so it doesn't look like you are fishing for one correct answer. For example, instead of asking, "What is the reason for high turnover in the early childhood profession?" ask "What are the reasons for high turnover in the early childhood field?" Using words like *might, some,* and *could* also signal that there are many possible responses to the question.

Directing questions

As you frame and ask a question, be clear in your own mind to whom the question is directed. If your intention is to elicit a response from anyone in the group, position your body open to the group and survey the entire audience with your eyes as you state the question. If you are directing it to a specific individual, face that person and make eye contact with him or her. In choosing how to direct questions, here are some things to consider.

Choosing How to Direct Questions

IF YOU WANT TO . . .	THEN . . .
Stimulate thinking	direct the question to the group.
Allow participants to respond voluntarily or avoid putting an individual on the spot	ask a question like, "What experiences have you had on this issue?"
Stimulate one person to think and respond	direct the question to that individual.
Tap the known resources of an "expert" in the group	direct the question to him or her: "Mary, you have had a lot of experience in completing the accreditation process, what would you do in this case?"

From Hart, L. (1991). Training methods that work: A handbook for trainers. Palo Alto, CA: Crisp Publications, p. 59. Reprinted with permission.

Sometimes a question bombs because it catches everyone by surprise. Timing is such a critical element in asking good questions. If you have directed a question to the entire group and no one responds, wait a full ten seconds and then rephrase the question. At that point, if you still do not have a volunteer response, you might call on someone who has previously been vocal in the group and whom you believe will not be caught off guard. You can say something like, "Monica, would you give us the benefit of your experience on this one?"

Beware of rhetorical questions. They are fine to use, but clearly signal in your voice that they are different from a question where you anticipate a response. In other words, don't confuse your audience in voice and body language. If you develop a certain style and rhythm to your presentation and if you use your body to cue the audience when you are shifting focus to ask a question where you expect a response, you will help your participants anticipate when you are genuinely soliciting their ideas and when you are merely making a statement in the form of a rhetorical question.

Answering Questions

Just as it takes real skill to frame and ask good questions, there is also an art to seeking good questions from workshop attendees. Prepare your participants for your expectations about asking questions in the opening ten minutes of your workshop. Inform them that you encourage and expect questions, and share your guidelines for asking questions. In order to do this, you need to first think through how you want to handle questions from the group.

When is the best time for you to answer questions? Some presenters prefer to have a designated time slot in their workshop devoted to answering questions; others are open to questions at any time during their presentation. Some trainers find that a brief question-and-answer session is a good transition immediately after a break. It can serve as a way to clear up any confusion about the material that was just presented and pave the way for a new topic that's about to unfold. There is no one right way to approach the issue of timing. The key is that you communicate your expectations to the group early in your session.

Unless you have warmed up your group to asking questions, you may find that your first invitation for questions puts people on the spot — their heads go down and they start taking notes. In a room full of strangers, it is only the most confident, extroverted person who has the courage to stand up and ask a question. If you feel your group may need some warming up to ask questions, an alternative strategy is to ask participants to generate questions in their table groupings. You can then ask each group to share one question of general interest with the entire group.

If you have a particularly large group — more than 75 participants — people may feel too intimidated to ask a question with all eyes focused on them. To encourage question asking in this situation, provide a supply of Post-it Notes at each table and encourage people to write down their questions. During the break, they can post them on a flip chart titled "What's on Your Mind?" positioned in the front of the room. You can then use those questions to get the discussion rolling.

Although it is not so critical how you structure the time for asking questions during your session, try to avoid ending your workshop with a question-and-answer session. People remember what they heard last in a workshop. Because you want to be in control of the final impressions people form as they leave your workshop, situate your final question-and-answer session before your closing remarks. That way participants will leave with your inspirational words on their mind, not someone's question that may not be relevant to their interests.

How you respond to the first question that is asked in your workshop is critical because it sets the tone for the group, letting them know how serious you are about being open to questions. It also allows you an opportunity to establish your answering style. Here are a few things you will want to think about:

- **Before you respond to a question, ask yourself, "Why is this person asking this question at this time?"** Discerning a person's motivation for asking a question can help you frame an appropriate response. What are the underlying feelings that may be prompting the question? Listen for the person's intent as well as what he or she is actually saying. Watch how the question is asked. Are there strong nonverbal cues that may communicate something deeper about the nature of the question and the questioner?

- **Think about how your response will affect the learning climate of the workshop.** Be clear about the outcome you want to achieve. Do you want to validate the person's expertise, help shift their perspective on an issue, encourage additional questions from other people, or prompt people to think about something new that they haven't considered previously? How you answer any specific question has an impact on subsequent questions asked and on the connections that people make between prior learning and new knowledge.

- **Listen with your whole body.** Stop what you are doing and look at the person asking the question. Don't look at your notes, your overhead transparencies, the polish on your nails, or anything else. Give your undivided attention to the person asking the question. Be still, make eye contact, and listen attentively until the person has completely finished the question. Although you may have heard the same question 50 times before, you have not heard it from this participant. Your active listening communicates respect for the person. As the individual is talking, reflect your understanding through nodding, smiling, or grimacing as appropriate.

- **Pause before responding.** Before responding, pause and reflect on the question for at least five seconds before responding. Your pause communicates interest, thoughtfulness, and respect for the questioner. It also gives you time to think through an appropriate response.

- **Acknowledge and thank the person by name for their question.** "Claire, that is an interesting question." Paraphrase or rephrase the question to clarify your understanding of it and to make sure that everyone else heard it. The exception to this would be if the person spoke the question into a handheld microphone.

- **Ask for clarification if necessary.** If you did not understand the question, ask for clarification, "Would you elaborate on what you mean by low morale?" "Could you give an example of what you mean by neglect?"

- **Defer irrelevant questions for later.** Be gracious if a person asks an irrelevant question or one that is too specific to be of interest to the entire group. Just indicate that you will be happy to talk with him or her during the break. "Jeff, that is an interesting question, but I'm not sure it is germane to our discussion today. Let's chat during our 10 o'clock break." Never give a sarcastic response or a putdown, even if the question is ludicrous.

- **Answer the question concisely, completely, and accurately.** Short answers are more credible than long-winded ones. Don't go off on a tangent or use the opportunity to give a speech. Try to match your response to the scope of the information requested.

- **If you don't know the answer to the person's question, be forthright and admit it.** You'll be perceived as being more honest if you admit your limitations rather than trying to fake it. Admitting shortcomings can actually increase your credibility with the group. Indicate that you will get back with an answer if the questioner asked for information that you can locate after the workshop session. As an alternative, you can suggest resources where the person may be able to locate the answer independently.

- **Involve other participants in answering questions.** Even if you know the answer to a question, occasionally involve other participants in the answer if you can. This strategy is particularly effective when the questioner has posed a problem and there is no single solution.

The more people involved in the answer, the greater the investment in that segment of your workshop. "Marge has asked a provocative question. Is there anyone who would care to share their perspective on the issue?"

- **Establish a wait list.** If you have a number of people clamoring to ask a question, identify the next three people you plan to recognize. This helps those who are in queue to relax and focus on the discussion.

- **Use a concrete object to signal a person's turn.** One way to recognize questions and energize the group at the same time is to toss a soft ball or Koosh ball to the person asking the first question. That person can then decide whom to recognize next by tossing the ball to that individual.

- **Don't debate, even if you disagree.** If you disagree with a point that a person made, don't debate. Don't try to sell your position. Your job as workshop leader is to help extend thinking and encourage people to explore multiple points of view.

Helping Participants Process and Recall Information

In her books, veteran teacher educator Elizabeth Jones talks about the important distinction between growing teachers and training teachers. Workshop leaders who are grounded in a constructivist philosophy understand this distinction well. They know that teaching does not guarantee learning. If we are to help "grow" teachers from the inside out, we need to infuse numerous opportunities for participants to process and recall information, challenging old paradigms and applying new concepts and ideas.

The statistics on memory retention are pretty dismal. If people are told something once there is less than a 10% chance they will recall it in 30 days. If you reinforce your point six times, however, there is an 80% chance they will recall it a month later. While experts differ over the precise percentage of retention depending on the type of information being recalled and the initial conditions of learning, the point is still valid. The curve of forgetting is a pretty steep incline unless you reinforce concepts repeatedly during a workshop.

The key is to make a review of the material an integral part of your workshop design. Weave in opportunities for participants to think aloud and exchange ideas with other participants as well as time to reflect quietly on the personal significance of new information. Don't skimp on the debriefing time you allocate for the group activities you incorporate into your session. Allowing ample time to talk about what happened during a structured activity is very important. It is in the debriefing portion of the activity that participants have an opportunity to reflect on the personal relevance of the activity.

Adults do not learn from experience, they learn from the processing of experience.

Bob Garmston

In his book *Creative Training Techniques*, Bob Pike cautions about the pace at which new material is introduced. Participants need time to absorb and make sense of the concepts and ideas you have taught them before you introduce new concepts or ideas. Sometimes less can be more. Pike uses the analogy of pouring liquid through a funnel. If you try to pour too fast, the liquid spills over and is lost. As a presenter you need to be mindful of both your delivery rate and the amount of information you are delivering. It is a delicate balance.

There are many ways to help participants process and recall information during and after your workshop. The important thing is that you make it a conscious and integral part of your workshop design. Here are a few strategies you can use.

Bridging

As you bridge from one subtopic to another, take a few minutes to review what you have just covered, and then forecast where you are heading in the next section of your presentation. Bridging helps make your connections readily apparent to your participants.

Be mindful of the different learning styles that we discussed in Chapter 3. People organize information in different ways. Some prefer to get an overview of the material and see where the various parts fit. Others create the big picture as they go along, organizing chunks of information in ways that make sense. The way you bridge topics needs to accommodate both types of learners.

Mnemonics

Mnemonics are a useful strategy for increasing people's retention by linking the key points you have covered in your workshop with headline words, each beginning with the same letter or sound. You can also present your points so the first letter of each word forms an acronym. This can serve as a memory trigger. Here is a simple example for TEAM:

> **T**ogether
> **E**veryone
> **A**chieves
> **M**ore

Bright ideas

At the beginning of your workshop, distribute a handout called "Bright Ideas." You'll find an example in Appendix J. Encourage participants to keep a running record of ideas they can apply back at their work setting. This page can include any new applications they see for the content. Periodically during the session, structure opportunities for participants to share their bright ideas with one another.

Humans don't get ideas; they make ideas.

Art Costa

Journal reflections

Particularly in workshops that span several days, participants need some quiet time to reflect on the personal significance of issues being covered in the training. You can do this informally by just asking them to write on a blank piece of notebook paper about any aspect of the training that comes to mind, or more formally with a bound notebook and structured questions that stimulate thinking.

Appendix K is an example of a reflection page I use during a weeklong leadership training I conduct. I have the form printed on carbonized paper. During our break before dinner each evening, I ask participants to write a page reflecting on both the content and the process of the day. They turn these reflections in at dinner as their meal ticket. That gives me time in the evening to read them and make comments in the margins. I keep the carbon copy and return the original to the participant the following morning at breakfast.

Before I launch into my topic after breakfast, I review the previous day's training by referring to some patterns I have detected in the reflections. If there are some interesting insights individuals have made on their reflections that I feel should be shared with the entire group, I ask those people during breakfast if they would be willing to make a short comment.

I've found this is a particularly powerful way to personalize the training. This strategy gets people thinking about the deeper significance of issues being covered and creates a community of learners who support one another.

A letter to myself

Distribute a piece of paper to each participant. It can be ordinary notebook paper or fancy embossed stationery. Ask participants to write a letter to themselves summarizing the key points they want to be sure to remember from the workshop. Have them seal the envelopes and put their own names and addresses on the front. In the corner where the stamp will be affixed, have them note a date when they would like you to mail the letter to them (some time over the next six months or year).

A contract with myself

To help participants think about how they will apply the information they have learned about a particular topic you cover during your workshop, distribute Appendix L. It asks them to describe how they plan to use the information at their work setting, with whom they will share information they have learned, and how they plan to enhance their skills in this area when the workshop is over.

Learning partner interview

Working in pairs, have participants interview one another. They can use the following three questions or any others you come up with:

- ✔ What is one important thing you learned from today's workshop?
- ✔ What is one thing you would like to know more about?
- ✔ How will you use the information you have learned today when you return to your job?

The interviewer should listen attentively to the comments of the interviewee, probing for additional information as needed. After five minutes, have the pairs reverse roles. This activity is simple to conduct, yet it is quite powerful for helping participants appreciate the ideas of others.

Turn and tell

A variation of the learning partner activity just described is another activity you can do in pairs. This one is particularly good when time is tight. Ask each person in the twosome to turn and tell their partner the following: one idea they want to implement, the benefits of doing so, obstacles they may encounter, and resources they can turn to. You will be pleased to hear in your debriefing of this activity how many of the participants count on each other as resources if they encounter obstacles.

Ten questions

In small groups, have participants think of ten questions they could ask that would test a person's knowledge of the workshop topic. These should not be trick questions, but rather questions relating to facts and information that have been covered during the session. Have them write each question on a separate piece of 8 x 11 inch card stock. They should then write the 10 answers on pieces of card stock. (It is best to use one color of cardstock for the questions; another color for the answers.)

When participants have completed their task, have each group trade their stack of question and answer cards with another group. That group's task is to match each question with its corresponding answer. These can be posted on the wall with small pieces of Velcro or masking tape. Provide some time for all groups to survey the variety of question and answer cards that have been posted.

Swap shop

This activity my friend Laura Lipton uses frequently in her training. Have people individually reflect on their thinking and learning by writing down at least three specific tools, structures, or ideas they intend to try out. Next, have them mingle, swapping ideas with other participants. Their goal is to collect as many ideas as possible in the time allotted to bring back to their small group. Each group then shares all the ideas collected. Finally, ask people to individually sort through all the great ideas they've heard and identify the three most interesting to them.

Flypaper

This is a quick way to have people reflect on what they have learned during the workshop. It can be done at any point during the day, but is most effective just after you conclude a subtopic and are ready to move on to a new subtopic.

Distribute a piece of flypaper (Appendix M) to each person and give the directions, "I'd like you think about one new thing you've heard today that really stuck. Write your reflection on your piece of flypaper." If time permits, have a few people share their thoughts with the entire group.

Think tank

Distribute the think tank handout to each person (Appendix N) and give the following directions: "Think of something that raises a question in your mind. Think of something that is still hazy to you and needs to be clarified. Think of a point that has been made that you really agree with. Think of something you've heard today that you disagree with."

Critical incident

One of the most effective ways you can ensure that people apply and adapt the ideas covered in your training is to encourage them to stay connected with you following your workshop. I like to give my telephone number to participants and encourage them to share their good stories with me after the workshop has ended.

Toward the end of a workshop, I often ask participants to open their calendars and circle a day approximately 60 days later. I ask them to sit down on that date and write me a note of one or two paragraphs describing a critical incident that has occurred since the workshop ended. My only guideline is that the critical incident should be an example of how they have applied the concepts, ideas, or information covered during the training.

I distribute my address label and an envelope to each person to underscore the seriousness of my invitation. I also make the promise that I will send them an article when they send me their critical incident scenarios. Some of the best material I've used in my writing and training has come from the contributions made by participants in these critical incident letters.

Action plan

For training that is more intensive in nature where the anticipated outcome is a change of behavior or the direct application of new information, it is good to have people develop an action plan detailing their goals, action steps, resources needed, and evaluation markers. Appendix O is an example of an action plan I use in training with early childhood directors.

I don't suggest using an action plan like this, however, if there will not be any kind of follow-up or support given to participants when they leave your training. It is my experience that people leave trainings with high expectations of what they want to do or accomplish, but unless there is focused follow-up, those aspirations evaporate as soon as they see the stack of unopened correspondence and telephone calls awaiting them the day they return to their work. Action plans without support only cause people to feel guilty. This can undermine self-esteem.

Three dimensional constructions

Using art is a particularly effective way to tap the right side of the brain and get people to process information in new ways. As a closing activity for a workshop on organizational change, my colleague Teri Talan brings in baskets full of interesting art material — pipe cleaners, string, stickers, Popsicle sticks, sea shells, corks, plastic caps, cigar boxes, cardboard tubes, small figurines, tissue paper, colored markers, scissors, glue — and asks teams to create a three-dimensional construction conveying the key concepts of the training. Before she even gets the directions out of her mouth the groups dive into action. The animated conversation that follows as people discuss how to communicate abstract concepts through art is both entertaining and educational.

After 20 minutes, each group makes a formal presentation of their construction, providing a narrative interpretation of the key elements it symbolizes. The workshop participants then vote on the most original entry and prizes are awarded.

Navigating the Potholes — When Problems Occur

No doubt about it, Murphy's Law reigns in the world of workshop presentation. Problems *will* occur and there *will* be difficult participants to contend with. It goes with the territory. Just because you've come across a few potholes in the road doesn't mean your obligation to reinforce learning connections ends. It only means you have to be more resourceful than you would otherwise. How you survive these situations will depend on your level of preparedness, your flexibility, and of course, your sense of humor.

The key is not what participants know when they leave our session, but what they do with what they know.

Bob Garmston

My colleague Bernadette Herman tells the following story about a workshop she gave for a group of elementary school teachers:

> *I was addressing a group of one hundred or so teachers, seeking to get them fired up about differentiated learning. The topic was practical. I was confident in my ability to initiate a helpful discussion. My warm-up fizzled. I tried a different approach. Fizzle. The teachers sat there, arms folded, faces frozen expressionlessly, looking certifiably bored. So I shifted my attention to the other side of the auditorium. Another sea of folded arms and frozen faces. They weren't paying me enough. The clock wasn't moving. No one had warned me that just previous to my session the faculty had been told that all contract negotiations had been broken off and that indeed their anticipated settlement had slipped back to 0%. The teachers were instantly on strike, and I was instantly paying for it.*

When problems like this occur, you may need to make split-second decisions about what to do and how to intervene. In a recent article in the *Journal of Staff Development*, veteran trainer Joleen Killian offers some advice on how to handle problems relating to group dynamics. She says when things go wrong, you have essentially five options:

- ***Option 1:* Do nothing.** With this strategy you make a conscious effort not to respond and hope the group will recognize and resolve its own problem without your intervention.

- ***Option 2:* Present your observations.** Describe what is occurring in the group. In selecting this intervention, you hope to raise the group's consciousness of its behavior. Use descriptive, factual language that describes actual behaviors without finding fault. "I am noticing that three people in the group are talking most of the time. They have talked for 15 minutes." In this instance, you act as a mirror to help the group see its own actions.

- ***Option 3:* Describe your own feelings.** In describing your own feelings about a situation it is important that you not project those feelings on the group or assume the group feels the same. Use "I" statements. For example if the group seems to be stuck in a "griping" mode, you might say, "I feel frustrated. As a group you have identified many of the problems associated with this situation. I wonder if you are ready to move on now and discuss solutions to the problems you have identified."

- ***Option 4:* Ask for help.** With this strategy you are seeking clarification or assistance from participants regarding what is occurring. The clarification could relate to the content: "I am unsure of the focus of your discussion now. We started out talking about nonmonetary ways to reward teachers, but your discussion seems to have become sidetracked now to issues about licensing standards." Or the clarification could relate to process: "Help me understand why the group seems sluggish right now. You appear reluctant to talk."

- *Option 5:* **Direct or redirect the content or process.** In this level of intervention, you take a more directive approach to changing the interaction occurring based on your understanding of what is most beneficial for the group. For example, "There seems to be some dominating of the discussion at the moment. Some participants are having a hard time getting a word in. Let's stop and do a round-robin process to allow each person a chance to offer his or her opinion."

Knowing how and when to intervene to redirect the group dynamics of your workshop to better support learning comes with experience. The thing to remember is that every group is different. An intervention strategy that is effective with one group may bomb with another. That's why being a workshop leader is such a humbling experience. Your willingness to risk trying new approaches and your flexibility in dropping those that don't work is essential if you are to grow in your role.

Handling Difficult Participants

Not all participants are going to be cooperative, eager, and friendly. There will be those who challenge your authority, test your patience, and make you wonder why you're flipping transparencies on a sunny Saturday morning when you could be home gardening or taking a hike. Participants who are difficult to please, difficult to manage, and simply difficult to be around are a reality in the trainer's world. I once had a participant tell me right to my face that she almost didn't come to my workshop because my name was Paula. She didn't trust anyone named Paula because her Aunt Paula embezzled her parents out of their summer cottage. I didn't ask for details, and I'm certainly glad she had the courtesy to tell me at the end of the workshop and not the beginning.

Despite the emotional energy that difficult participants take, some of the most rewarding moments you'll experience as a trainer will be associated with those difficult people whom you were able to transform in some small way — the hostile participant who ends up writing the most glowing evaluation, or the disinterested, reluctant participant who leaves your workshop energized and revitalized. Here are some things to think about as you work with different types of difficult people.

The monopolizing type

Monopolizers have something to say about everything. Their hands pop up in response to a question you are about to ask before you've punctuated the sentence. They hog all available airtime if given the opportunity. The trick to handling monopolizers is that you don't want to dampen their enthusiasm; you just want to temper their dominating presence in the group.

There are some strategies you can use to let monopolizers know that they've said enough. Avoid eye contact, and direct questions away from them toward other members of the group. You can say, "Amy we've heard your perspective several times this morning. Are there others who would like to express their opinion on this issue?" If they don't get the hint and persist in posturing for attention, it may be necessary to speak privately with them to suggest the value of letting others participate.

The rambling type

People who ramble are often unaware of how they repeat themselves and digress from the main point they are trying to make. They have no idea how time is ticking away, how a simple response that should have taken less than a minute to make has stretched into five or six minutes.

This problem can usually be remedied by setting clear guidelines at the beginning of your workshop — the expectation that people will be both precise and concise when commenting before the whole group. If someone does ramble then, you can gently remind him or her to be more cognizant of the time constraints of the workshop. You can also designate a person in the group to serve as timer when an open discussion occurs. The timer can give a simple hand signal when a speaker's time has expired or pass a small hour glass as a visual reminder when a person's time is up.

The argumentative type

The most important thing to do when confronted with an argumentative or hostile participant is to try to discern the source of the hostility. Is there some confusion or frustration the person is experiencing that may be the source of their anger? Remember, not every hostile remark has a hostile intent. Some people just have a negative tone of voice or an inflection that gives their remarks a biting edge.

A hostile, argumentative, or irreverent remark is sometimes due to cognitive dissonance — when a person is trying to protect existing beliefs and prejudices by rejecting contradictory information. A teacher, for example, who has done worksheets and didactic drill activities with five-year-olds her entire teaching career may feel challenged and defensive when she learns about developmentally appropriate practices that are contrary to her behavior. A negative or hostile-sounding remark may also be due to the fact that a participant just does not understand the content. If you suspect this is the root of their argumentative posture, handle the situation carefully to allow the person to "save face." A shift in presentation is in order to support the person to better understand the content being covered.

It has been said that there are no hostile questions, only defensive answers. The key to dealing with an argumentative participant is to avoid being drawn into an argument. Pause before responding to a hostile question to allow yourself time to think about your answer. Remember, the other participants will be looking at you and watching how you handle the situation. They are more interested in your tone and how you treat the person than what you actually say. Avoid sounding defensive and never use sarcasm or biting humor in response to a hostile question. A flippant remark can antagonize a hostile person and create a real power struggle. Instead, use phrases like "I see where you are coming from," or "I appreciate your perspective." As an alternative, reflect back a hostile question to the whole group and ask if anyone in the group would like to respond. Often a response coming from a participant will dissipate the anger compared to the same response coming from a trainer who may be perceived as an authority figure.

The disruptive type

Sometimes there are participants who see your workshop as an opportunity to socialize with their friends and catch up on news. They may engage in side chatter, return late from breaks, or laugh inappropriately at different points during the training. One of my colleagues once had a woman in her workshop take off her shoes and perch her feet on the table. She then opened a bag of potato chips and begin to eat them. It is important early in your training to stem this kind of behavior or it can sabotage your workshop goals.

If you notice that people have clustered in cliques as they arrive, make sure in your first interactive exercise you group people in such a way as to break up the clique. This in itself can change the group dynamic and reduce disruptive behavior. It may be necessary to remind the group of their collective responsibility for making the workshop a success. You may also want to repeat the ground rules of showing mutual respect, returning from breaks on time, and working collaboratively. If these strategies fail, speak to the disruptive participants separately during a break and encourage them to reflect on their behavior.

The disinterested type

You can spot the disinterested type easily. That glazed look of boredom, the wide-mouthed yawn, and the arms folded across the chest are obvious clues that the person was probably required to attend your workshop and did not come voluntarily. The opening ten minutes of your session are critical for converting the disinterested person. Stress the personal benefits to be gained in your workshop. If possible try to direct a question or two specifically at the disinterested person to get him or her involved. You might even ask the person to assist you in recording ideas on a flip chart or distributing handouts. Sometimes all it takes is a bit of personal attention to transform a disinterested person into an enthusiastic and eager participant.

If those strategies don't work or if you discover, as Bernadette did, that the entire room is full of disinterested types, you may need to do something more radical. You can say something like, "I'm really sorry you were required to attend this session and you don't want to be here. Perhaps we can arrive at a mutually satisfactory agreement. If you will remain open-minded and patient, I will do my utmost to make this an engaging, interesting, and worthwhile experience for you." Sometimes confronting the behavior openly like this can clear the air and provide a fresh start.

The complainer

You've met the complainer — the coffee is cold, the seats are too hard, there aren't enough breaks, and oh by the way, why aren't there croissants instead of bagels? I even had a woman complain once that there were too many sesame seeds on the bun of her vegetarian sandwich. And I was feeling pretty proud that I'd gone out of my way to order a few vegetarian selections for the event. She gave new meaning to the term "personal attention."

I'm not sure there is any surefire strategy for handling complaints about sesame seeds. I think it is important, however, to listen attentively and respond courteously to the complainer's comments. Respond politely, but don't couch your response as an excuse. Complainers of the nitpicking variety don't care about your explanation. Simply thank them for their suggestions and tell them you'll consider their comments seriously as you work to improve your workshop next time.

Remember, though, not all complaints are frivolous. When a person makes a legitimate complaint about some facet of your workshop that needs improving, try to involve the person or the group in solving the problem. While this strategy is time intensive, it helps the individual and the group solve their own problems. It also helps them see the big picture of what it takes to put on a smooth functioning workshop.

For example, I recently had a woman complain during the morning break at one of my workshops about the amount of noise generated when the small groups were working simultaneously. I viewed her complaint as a legitimate concern. I explained to her that we did not have the option of having some of the groups work in a different room or in the hallway. This would have solved the problem but the conference facility would have levied a hefty surcharge to do so. After the break I brought the issue before the entire group for their deliberation. It took 10 minutes away from the training, but the time was well worth it. The group came up with an alternative grouping strategy that helped decrease the noise level. As a result, the woman's attitude about the workshop changed dramatically and the group felt more empowered by the experience.

Spice Up Your Presentation with Visuals

The old adage "A picture is worth a thousand words" has taken on new meaning in recent years as research from the neurosciences has confirmed the importance of visual stimuli for receiving and retrieving information. There are seven times as many human brain cells devoted to visual processing as there are to hearing and touch. It is estimated that people gain 75% of what they know visually, 13% through auditory channels, and only 12% through smell, touch, and taste combined. These scientific findings confirm what we all know from personal experience — that it is easier to recall information if we have visual stimuli to trigger the memory process.

While it will always be true that you are your own best audiovisual aid, good trainers understand the power and potency of using a variety of visual aids in their workshops. These can include handouts, overhead transparencies, slides, videotapes, flip charts, computer-assisted instruction, and props. Even if you are planning a workshop of only an hour in length, your participants will benefit from visual aids.

In this chapter you'll learn the basics of why visual aids are important and how to use them effectively in your workshop. You'll learn tips for creating handouts that participants save and refer to after your workshop is over, guidelines for making transparencies and slides that attract and retain attention, suggestions on how to use videos effectively, and techniques for creating memorable flip charts. The chapter concludes with some thoughts about computer-assisted presentations and suggestions on how props can enliven your workshop.

Why Use Visual Aids?

Visual aids keep people's brains engaged while you are talking. The typical trainer speaks about 100 to 200 words per minute, but people can think at a much faster rate of 400 to 500 words per minute. Even when they're sitting in the workshop of a fast talker, that still leaves a lot of extra time for the mind to click channels and start planning that upcoming birthday party. Providing visual stimuli while you are talking helps the brain stay connected to you and your message.

Visual aids can help

- ✔ focus the attention of participants
- ✔ reinforce verbal messages
- ✔ add variety
- ✔ emphasize main points
- ✔ create a common frame of reference
- ✔ decrease the likelihood of misunderstanding
- ✔ increase retention

As a presenter you may think your description of a point is crystal clear, but seeing it in print or conveyed in a graphic image ensures that people understand it the way you intended. This is particularly important in workshops with technical jargon or complex information.

Visual aids are not only important for your participants, they can also serve as a valuable tool for you. They can substitute for your notes, serving as a prompter or road map to guide your presentation. This can boost your confidence because you are freed from the mental chains of your note cards.

If you are a novice workshop presenter, you'll quickly appreciate the value of visual aids because they take the focus off of you. This can help reduce your level of anxiety and nervousness. I remember when I first starting making presentations, my favorite workshop topic was learning environments. The reason was that the first portion of my workshop involved a slide presentation. As the lights dimmed, my confidence grew. The participants' attention was diverted from me to the sensational slides I had taken of indoor and outdoor learning environments. I could speak enthusiastically and confidently while the lights were off. By the time the slide presentation finished, I was warmed up and confident, no longer nervous or worried about how I was coming across as a presenter.

In her book *Graphics for Presenters*, Lynn Kearny provides some useful tips on determining which visual aids are most appropriate. She suggests preparing the content of your workshop first without regard to visuals. Then ask yourself if a visual aid would be helpful in clarifying any portion of your content. If so, then decide what type of aid would be most effective. The key is that the visual aid you decide on should be

- ✔ simple
- ✔ legible
- ✔ accurate
- ✔ colorful
- ✔ manageable
- ✔ meaningful

Kearney stresses that visual aids need to support your specific workshop objectives; they shouldn't be eye-catching substitutes for boring training material. The information in each visual should relate directly to the point you make verbally in your training, leaving no confusion in the minds of your participants. That means any color code, symbol, or lettering key should be visually displayed in the same manner in which you verbally describe it during your workshop.

Handouts

If you want to win over the hearts of early childhood educators, you'd better include handouts in your workshop. There is something about trekking home with a packet of handouts that serves as a powerful symbol of professional growth and development. Early childhood folks love them. Handouts are important for several reasons:

- **Handouts supplement your teaching.** The participants in your session can't possibly take accurate notes on everything you cover. Handouts can help by summarizing key points and information.

- **Handouts fill gaps of knowledge and information.** There may be topics you can only cover superficially in the time allotted for your workshop. Handouts can serve to fill these gaps in knowledge or information.

- **Handouts help you prepare for your presentation**. In order to compile a packet of handouts, you need to review and become thoroughly familiar with the material you will be covering in your workshop. The process helps ensure you are organized and prepared for your session.

- **Handouts can enhance your reputation.** A well-designed packet of handouts can serve as a marketing tool. When participants go back to their own centers or share workshop information with colleagues at other centers, your reputation as a first-rate trainer will spread.

Types of handouts

While handouts are dandy, too many handouts can overwhelm participants and cause a negative reaction to your workshop. People can only digest so much during the course of your workshop. Strive for quality, not quantity. The key is to determine what people need to know within the scope of your workshop topic and judiciously and carefully select handouts that support and enrich your workshop.

There are several different types of handouts you may want to include in your session. Each serves a different purpose. The key is to be selective about handouts, using only those that serve a useful purpose.

- **Summary material.** Summary materials are outlines, graphs, charts, models, or bulleted points you make during your session. Often they are paper copies of transparencies or slides you show. Their purpose is to serve as a convenient way for participants to organize note taking and as a reference of important ideas and concepts when your workshop is over. Here is a summary handout from a workshop on performance appraisal.

Implementing an Effective Performance Appraisal System

USING MULTIPLE SOURCES OF EVIDENCE

- Standardized rating forms

- Feedback from parents

- Feedback from fellow teachers

- Self assessment

- Videotaped segments of classroom instruction

- Artifacts and examples of professional activities

- Journal reflections

Paula Jorde Bloom, The Center for Early Childhood Leadership

5

● **Instructions.** You may plan an activity during your workshop session that requires participants to do certain things or follow certain steps. To facilitate your verbal instructions, written instructions are often helpful to include as a handout. Having written instructions that people can read helps those who do not process directions well auditorily. Visual learners particularly appreciate written instructions. Here is an example of a team assignment.

Circle of Influence

WORK TEAM ASSIGNMENT

What are some of the ways that a director can nurture trust and a spirit of collaboration?

• Generate as many ideas as possible. Try to be as specific as possible.

• Assign a scribe to record your ideas on flip chart paper.

• For the debriefing, select two ideas to share with the entire group.

8

Paula Jorde Bloom, The Center for Early Childhood Leadership

Another occasion when you might need instructions is if you assign different roles for a role play activity. Written scripts or role play scenarios that participants read can help them play their roles more authentically.

- **Fill-in materials.** During the course of your workshop, you may want participants to write a reflection, take a short quiz, or complete a brief assessment. The purpose of fill-in handouts is to serve as a teaching tool during your session. These handouts are supplemented by your verbal instructions. The following fill-in handout is one I use for a workshop on the topic of interpersonal communication.

Promoting Effective Communication

THINK ABOUT . . .

an incident you may have had recently where you felt you were misunderstood. Reconstruct the situation from your perspective. Why do you think you were misunderstood? What was the short-term consequence of this encounter on your relationship with the other individual? Could the misunderstanding have been avoided?

_____

_____

_____

_____

_____

THINK ABOUT . . .

a relationship in which you have developed a high level of trust. What are the factors that promote trust in this relationship?

_____

_____

_____

_____

_____

_____

3

Paula Jorde Bloom, The Center for Early Childhood Leadership

- **Informational materials.** Informational materials supplement important information you cover in your workshop providing more depth about specific issues or topics that you mention. The purpose of informational handouts is to serve as additional information for participants to read when the workshop is over. They can be articles, fact sheets, abstracts, or activities and strategies that participants can apply in their work setting. The following is an example of an informational handout.

Circle of Influence

CONSENSUS-BUILDING STRATEGIES

You and your staff can tackle tough issues by using a variety of consensus-building techniques and avoiding other decision-making methods that result in dividing the staff into winners and losers. Here are a few you can consider:

- **Finger voting.** Group members hold up fingers to indicate the level of their support.
  - *Five fingers:* Total agreement, best solution, complete support
  - *Four fingers:* Agree, good solution, support
  - *Three fingers:* Okay with me, willing to support
  - *Two fingers:* Don't agree, not my choice, but I can live with it
  - *One finger:* No way, let's think of an alternative

- **Negative voting.** When several solutions to a problem are proposed, ask individuals to indicate which options they could not live with. Eliminate those that are unacceptable, and focus on the choices with the least opposition.

- **Essential features.** Identify the elements of each proposal that the staff agree with. Use these as the basis for generating other agreements, combinations, or acceptable refinements of the original proposals.

- **Plus-and-minus tally.** Write each alternative on a separate sheet of flip chart paper. Staff members can then discuss and list the positive (+) aspects of each proposal and the negative (-) aspects.

- **Rank order.** Have group members write each alternative on a separate slip of paper. Ask them to arrange their slips in order - from most desirable to least desirable. The slips of paper can then be collected and tallied.

- **Dot voting.** Alternatives generated from a group discussion are written on flip chart paper and posted on the wall. Each staff member gets 5 to 8 dot stickers. They can use these dots to "vote" for the ideas listed, even placing more than one sticker next to an item they feel particularly strong about.

10

Paula Jorde Bloom, The Center for Early Childhood Leadership

Be careful you don't overload participants with informational handouts. They must be compelling enough to ensure that they will be of interest to the participants once they leave the workshop. Know the educational level of your audience and vary the handouts to meet the needs of the entire group.

- **Resources.** Resource materials supplement your workshop by providing useful information for participants regarding bibliographic references or a listing of sources for supplies, equipment, and educational materials. When you put together resource handouts, be selective about what you include. List only those books and suggested readings that you can personally recommend. Participants don't want a bibliography that you photocopied out of some textbook. They want recommendations based on your personal knowledge of the topic. Likewise, when you compile a list of resources, double check that the addresses and phone numbers are complete and current. There is nothing more deflating than trying to track down a resource listed on a workshop handout that is outdated. Here is an example of a handout of suggested supplementing reading I compiled for a workshop on stress management.

Managing Stress and Avoiding Burnout

SUPPLEMENTAL READING

Baldwin, S. (1996). *Lifesavers: Tips for success and sanity.* Stillwater, MN: Insights Training.

Ban Breathnach, S. (1995). *Simple abundance: A day book of comfort and joy.* New York: Time Warner.

Bloom, P. J. (1982). *Avoiding burnout: Strategies for managing time, space, and people in early childhood education.* Lake Forest, IL: New Horizons.

Carlson, R. (1997). *Don't sweat the small stuff.* New York: Hyperion.

Davidson, J., (1991). *Breathing space: Living and working at a comfortable pace in a sped-up society.* New York: MasterMedia Ltd.

Gellens, S. (1994, September). Paralyzed by personal stress: A director's story. *Child Care Information Exchange,* 11-14.

Greenman, J. (1994, July). Looking for high ground: Balancing needs of children, staff, and parents. *Child Care Information Exchange,* 11-14.

Gruenberg, A. (1998, January). Creative stress management: "Put your own oxygen mask on first." *Young Children,* 38-42.

Hochschild, A. (1997). *The time bind: When work becomes home and home becomes work.* New York: Metropolitan Books.

Rechtschaffen, S. (1996). *Time shifting: Creating more time to enjoy your life.* New York: Doubleday.

St. James, E. (1996). *Living the simple life: A guide to scaling down and enjoying more.* New York: Hyperion.

Weil, A. (1997). *Eight weeks to optimum health.* New York: Knopf.

18

Paula Jorde Bloom, The Center for Early Childhood Leadership

Creating and assembling handouts

In the world of public relations, it goes without saying that packaging is everything. The same marketing principles apply to the packet of handouts you create for your workshop. The appearance of your handouts is a direct reflection of your professionalism. Make sure they project the image you want. Here are a few tips to consider:

- **Strive for consistency in the appearance.** Use the same typeface and font size throughout. Put a heading on each page. It can be in caps or upper and lower case, but use the same style on all pages. Orient the text on pages similarly — either vertically (portrait orientation) or horizontally (landscape orientation) — to prevent participants from having to turn their handouts in different directions to read.

- **Create a distinctive trademark.** Create a personal logo, emblem, or graphic that you can add to your handouts to be a distinctive trademark for your materials. This need not be something costly or fancy; even a unique border can be your personal signature statement.

- **Proofread, proofread, and proofread.** And when you are done, proofread one more time. Make sure there are no typographic errors anywhere in your handouts.

- **Number the bottom of each page.** Assemble the pages in your packet in the order in which you will be using the handouts, and number consecutively. During the session you can refer to the page numbers to help people follow along. Add extra note-taking pages at the end of your packet.

- **Use color paper to create a special effect.** Add variety and increase interest by putting your handouts on light color paper. Cream, buff, beige, light green, grey, sky blue, or any of the natural earth tones are good shades to choose from. Avoid fluorescent or bold colors. They tire the eyes. Consider color coding different sections of your handout packet. This adds cost, but it facilitates referencing subtopics.

- **Create a customized cover.** Print your cover on color card stock and include a graphic that relates to your topic. Include your name, title, contact information, and the date and location of your presentation.

- **Bind your packet.** Although it increases the cost of production, binding your handouts gives them a professional appearance. Consider cloth tape binding or plastic spiral binding. Alternatively, you can staple the pages together in the top left-hand corner or three hole punch the pages so participants can insert them into a binder.

Don't just leave pages loose unless you have only a few handouts. If you have fewer than five sheets of paper in total, you can paper clip them together or insert them in a folder. Loose pieces of paper usually translate to lost training time. Some participants invariably misplace pages and take extra time locating replacements.

- **Make sure copies are smudge free.** Check the first set of handouts that comes out of the photocopy machine to make sure they do not have stray marks or smudges. If you are making a photocopy of a journal or magazine article, track down the original. Do not make a copy of a copy of a copy. Your participants will toss out blurry reproductions, and you will have wasted your time and money.

Copyright issues

In compiling your training materials, pay careful attention to copyright issues. If you want to use something from a copyrighted source, be sure to contact the author or copyright holder and get permission to reproduce and distribute it at your workshop. Allow plenty of lead time to acquire releases. Most copyright holders will not charge you a fee to distribute material for training purposes unless you are selling your handouts. When you have acquired permission to reprint, indicate the original source on the bottom of your handout along with any special notation required by the copyright holder. If you have modified or adapted from another source, indicate this on the bottom of your handout.

When you develop original material yourself, be sure to show a credit line on the cover of your handouts by displaying the © symbol, your name, and the year the material was created. This is important because participants may share your handouts with others. You want to make sure you are credited for your hard work. Your training materials are automatically protected when you create them. It is not necessary to formally register with the copyright office to secure copyright privileges; however, you may choose to do so.

Distributing handouts

Distribute handout packets to participants as they enter your workshop. This gives them time to glance through the material prior to the beginning of the session and begin thinking about some of the issues you will be covering. Some presenters disagree with this approach because they feel it takes away from the surprise element of presenting each new handout fresh. If your goal is to facilitate learning, however, even a few minutes to preview the materials can help serve as an advance organizer for the day.

If there are a few selected handouts you want viewed with fresh eyes, these can be held out of the workshop packet and distributed at the time they are needed. When distributing handouts during your session, try to do it in such a way that it does not slow the momentum of your workshop. Distribute the handouts while participants are engaged in another activity, or have someone assist you to expedite the process. Just make sure you don't create aimless dead time while this task is being carried out.

A final and important thought about handouts. Never give participants something to read and then read it to them. Most people want handouts that supplement what they've learned.

Overhead Transparencies

Using an overhead projector and transparencies is a surefire way to increase visual variety in your workshop. This visual aid has strong appeal to trainers because workshop participants like looking at projected images of key concepts and important information. When you mention three important points and are able to show those same points as a projected image, their importance is underscored and your credibility is enhanced. In her excellent book *Sharing Your Good Ideas*, Peggy Sharp summarizes the advantages of using overhead transparencies:

- ✔ Overhead transparencies can be used with any size group.
- ✔ Operating an overhead projector takes little technical skill.
- ✔ Because the lights stay on, participants can see both you and your visual.
- ✔ Overhead projectors are usually provided at no cost to presenters at conferences.
- ✔ Overhead transparencies are flexible. They can be easily rearranged as the content and participants require.
- ✔ Overhead transparencies can be written on while they are projected, allowing for modifications as additional information is shared.
- ✔ Overhead transparencies are easy to transport.
- ✔ Overhead transparencies can be easily updated and replaced.

Sharp also points out a few disadvantages of using an overhead projector and transparencies:

- ✔ The fans on some projectors make a distracting hum. This can be annoying to both you and your participants.
- ✔ The quality of the projected image depends on the quality of the machine.
- ✔ Poor lighting conditions in a room can make a projected image look washed out.

Creating eye-catching transparencies

Poor examples of transparencies abound. No doubt you've suffered through workshops, as I have, where the type size on a projected transparency was so small it couldn't be read past the first row; where the image was so smudged it looked like a cat walked over it with muddy paws; and where the sheer weight of the text made you feel as if you were reading a dissertation abstract. This need not be the case.

Computer programs now make it easy to create customized transparencies for your workshop. You can print transparencies directly from most laser jet and ink jet printers, or you can use your original paper copy to make a transparency using a photocopier or color copier. In creating your transparencies, here are some guidelines to follow:

- **Keep your transparencies simple.** Limit the information on each transparency to a single idea. Follow the six-by-six rule: no more than six lines and six words per line. Pretend you are writing a headline and use the fewest words possible to communicate your message. Avoid using abbreviations, however. The actual words or phrases you use may not make sense alone, but that is okay. Your role as presenter is to explain the information. The purpose of your headline is merely to create a shorthand phrase to capture your idea.

THE DIRECTOR AS CHANGE AGENT

- Serves as a catalyst for change

- Articulates a vision for change

- Creates a climate for change

- Provides resources and encouragement

- Manages and protects time

- **Order the information logically**. Put your points in the order you will be talking about them. Don't include information you don't plan to talk about. Double check that you have not made any errors in grammar, spelling, or punctuation.

- **Use number and bullets to list items.** Use numbers when you want to order items sequentially, rank items, or indicate a hierarchy of importance. Use bullets, check marks, boxes, or arrows when you want to indicate the items are of equal weight.

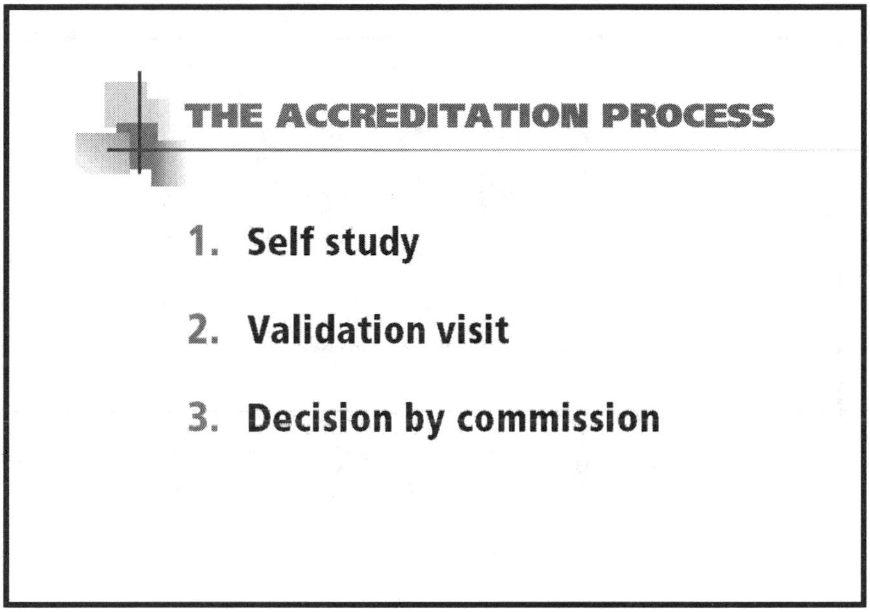

THE ACCREDITATION PROCESS

1. Self study

2. Validation visit

3. Decision by commission

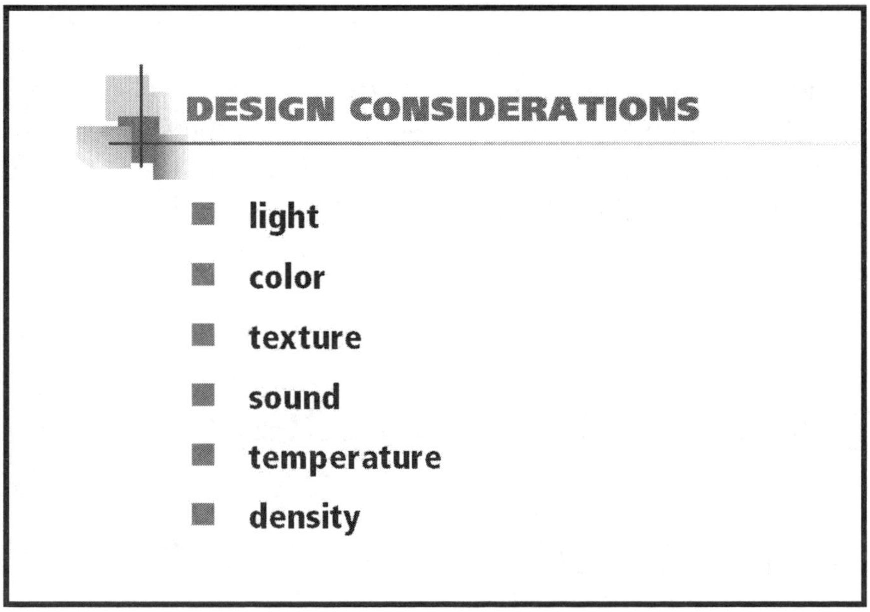

DESIGN CONSIDERATIONS

- light
- color
- texture
- sound
- temperature
- density

- **Make the focal point of your transparency obvious.** Arrange the text and graphics in such a way that it is clear where you want the eye to be drawn. Divide the space on your transparency in an interesting manner to create visual variety. Leave ample white space and use the same spacing between items.

In organizations where everyone
thinks alike, no one thinks very much.
Walter Lippmann

- **Make your title or headline larger than the text.** Use 24-point type or larger for your title and 18-point type or larger for your text. You can vary the type size in order to illustrate the relative importance of the information, but don't use more than three type sizes on any one transparency. Some trainers use all capital letters for their titles and upper- and lowercase letters for their text. Decide on your own personal style and be consistent on all transparencies.

An example of 18-point lettering

An example of 24-point lettering

- **Use color to create impact.** Used appropriately and purposefully, color can add impact to your message. Different colors evoke different emotions, however, so select your colors carefully. Limit your choice of colors to no more than three on any one transparency, make sure they don't clash, and use colors that are consistent with the message you are communicating. Try to keep the color theme consistent on all the transparencies you are using for a particular workshop. Strive for a strong contrast between the text color and the background color. Transparencies with dark text on a light background are easier to read than white or light-color text on a dark background. Concentrate bright colors in the areas that you want to receive the most attention.

- **Select a type style that is easy to read.** Your typeface also needs to be consistent with the message in your text. You wouldn't want to use a frilly, swirling type style, for example, for text on a serious topic like child abuse and neglect. Don't use more than two typefaces on any one transparency, and try to use the same typeface on all your transparencies to provide consistency. The following examples are popular choices for transparencies.

Serif Typefaces

This is an example of Courier New

This is an example of Times New Roman

This is an example of Book Antiqua

Sans Serif Typefaces

This is an example of Helvetica

This is an example of Century Gothic

This is an example of Tahoma

- **Use bold lettering.** Bold lettering will help the participants in the back of the room read your transparencies. Use italic print and underlining for emphasis, but use them sparingly. Consider using drop shadows to highlight words or text. This special effect can add depth to your visuals.

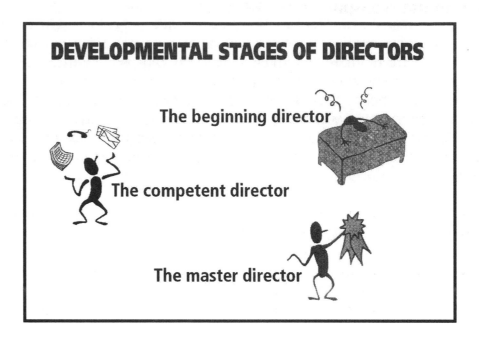

DEVELOPMENTAL STAGES OF DIRECTORS

The beginning director

The competent director

The master director

- **Use graphics to boost visual appeal.** With the abundance of public domain clip art now available, it is easy to create transparencies that include interesting images and clever graphics. Make sure the graphic images you use support your message, however, and don't clutter your visual.

- **Be consistent in the format of your transparencies.** Some presenters prefer a horizontal orientation because it allows more text to be written across. Others prefer a vertical orientation. Which orientation you choose is a matter of personal preference. The important thing is to use the same orientation for all transparencies in any given workshop. That way you won't need to make any changes in the screen position.

- **Preserve your transparencies.** To make sure your transparencies won't get damaged, put a piece of paper between transparencies when you store them. To increase the durability of your transparencies, you may want to mount them on plastic or cardboard frames. This prevents the acetate from curling and provides you with a space for making marginal notes. More important, the frame blocks the band of light that is visible around the edges when the transparency is projected. The downside to frames is that they add bulk and are more difficult to transport. As an alternative, you can tape off a frame on the overhead projector. That will help you position your transparencies while also blocking the light.

How to use transparencies like a pro

Now that you know how to create eye-catching transparencies, you may be tempted to mass produce them for your next workshop. Temper your enthusiasm. If you bombard your participants with too many visuals, you'll diminish their impact. People can absorb only so much visual stimulation. Veteran trainer Bob Garmston recommends no more than seven overheads for a 50-minute talk. He says each transparency, even if it contains no more than one picture or half a dozen key words, is usually enough for five to ten minutes of speaking.

Looking and feeling like a pro when you use transparencies will come with practice. Here are a few tips to get you started.

- **Learn to control the projector lamp.** Place your transparency on the projector glass before you turn it on, otherwise the lamp will project a blinding light. Likewise, when you finish showing your last transparency, turn the projector off before you remove the transparency from the machine. Your audience will appreciate this. Remove your transparency or cover it up when you have finished talking about it. This will help refocus the participants' attention from the screen back to you.

  Some presenters turn the projector off before removing a transparency and then on again when they have positioned their new transparency. A lot of participants find this technique annoying. An alternative is to put your new transparency into the light beam above the glass while you simultaneously remove the old one. With a bit of practice, this procedure comes across as far more smooth and professional than clicking the projector on and off.

- **Highlight information with a water-soluble color marker.** Use markers while you are discussing a transparency to circle, underline, or check off items you are talking about. This helps keep your audience's attention. If your transparencies correspond to pages in your handout packet, you can use a water-soluble pen to write the page number on the transparency of the corresponding handout page. This helps people follow along without your having to mention the handout page each time you project a new image. After your presentation you can wipe your transparencies with a damp cloth to remove the marker.

- **Use a pointer.** There are some clever and humorous pointers you can purchase from trainer supplies catalogues. I have one that looks like a small hand with a finger pointing. It never fails to get a few chuckles when I place it on the projector. You can also make your own pointers out of dark construction paper.

- **Use transparency overlays.** This technique is particularly effective when you have complex information to communicate — too much to put on one transparency. Create a series of transparencies with different parts of the complete image. As you talk about each part, put it on top of the previous image. Building the information slowly like this allows time for participants to absorb the information and see the relationship of the information you are presenting.

- **Reveal items.** Another technique you can use is to reveal items on the transparency as you discuss them. Use a piece of heavy paper to cover the items on the transparency you have not yet discussed. As you disclose information, slide the paper to reveal the next item. If there is a chance the paper will fly off the projector, wedge it between the transparency and the projector glass.

Slides

You can talk about children, classrooms, and the elements of a high-quality educational experience, but seeing real-life examples of good teaching in action will help your audience internalize the important concepts you share. Slides allow your audience to experience vicariously the issues you are talking about. They bring to life the important points you make. Peggy Sharp summarizes the advantages of this visual aid when she writes,

- ✔ Slides can be easily seen by large groups.
- ✔ Slides can give the participants a clearer understanding of what you are describing because they show real people in real situations.
- ✔ It is fairly easy to make professional-looking slides
- ✔ After the slides are arranged in the projector, showing them is simply a matter of turning the projector on and pressing the advance button.
- ✔ It is easy to rearrange slides as the content and participants require.

Sharp also points out some of the limitations of this visual aid:

- ✔ Slides are most effective in a completely darkened room, making eye contact between the presenter and participants impossible — and participants' reactions difficult to monitor.
- ✔ There is usually little interruption and discussion until the slides are finished and the lights are turned on again.
- ✔ Slides tend to jam in the projector.
- ✔ Remote control mechanisms are not sturdy or reliable.
- ✔ When a bulb burns out in the projector, the machine has to be opened in the middle of a presentation and the bulb removed in order to get a new light source.

Organizing and presenting slides

Even with the limitations that this medium presents, many trainers are still enthusiastic about using slides to showcase important ideas in their workshops. Here are some tips should you decide to join their ranks:

- **Code your slides.** As you prepare your slide presentation, number, label, or code your slides with a small color stripe or dot to aid in organizing your images. Your code will also serve as a quick prompter of the correct positioning of the slide should it fall out of the carousel slide tray. Because I have close to a thousand slides depicting different aspects of early childhood programming, I have color coded my slides along the top edge of each. A purple stripe, for example, is my code for outdoor play spaces; an orange stripe is my code for infant environments.

- **Use a carousel slide tray for 80 slides.** The smaller capacity trays that accommodate 80 instead of 140 slides are better for slide presentations because the slides don't get stuck as often. For this reason, some trainers prefer using plastic mounts instead of the less-expensive cardboard mounts. Don't forget to secure the plastic lock ring on top of the tray once the slides have been loaded. And learn how to remove the tray should a slide jam.

- **Use all horizontal or all vertical slides.** Using the same orientation will be less confusing for your participants as they watch the images projected on the screen. It also allows you to position the projector at the beginning of your presentation and know the projected image placement on the screen will work for the entire presentation.

- **Preview from different vantage points.** Before your participants arrive, sit in the back row and imagine that a person is sitting in front of you. Can you still see the projected image? Make sure you have the projector positioned so that it creates the largest image possible, filling up the screen.

- **Use black filler slides.** Use black filler slides so your participants won't be blinded by the bright light projecting on the screen. Black filler slides placed before your first slide and after your last slide help ensure a smoother beginning and ending to your presentation. Another way to remedy the light problem is to turn off the overhead lights in the room after you have projected your first image. At the end of your presentation, keep you last image projected while you turn the overhead lights back on.

- **Leave a dim light on in the room.** It is both disorienting and difficult for people to listen to you if they are in a totally darkened room. A dim light helps participants keep connected to you, but the light should not be so bright that it affects the projected image.

- **Stand in front of your audience**. As you present your slides, stand in front of your audience to the side of the screen and use a remote control to operate the slide projector. This positioning helps your audience stay connected to you and be better able to hear you.

- **Vary your pace.** Change slides about once every ten to twenty seconds, but add some variety to your pacing, otherwise your rhythm may become monotonous. Pause immediately after you've projected a new image. This gives your audience a moment to absorb and understand the new image without trying to listen to you at the same time. Never leave an image projected longer than is necessary. People need to be able to view the image on each slide long enough to form an impression and make connections with previous slides they've seen, but not so long that the image becomes stale. You can estimate the total length of your presentation by multiplying the number of slides you have by the average time you anticipate spending on each slide. Be sure to factor in time for questions if your style is to allow interruptions during your slide presentation.

- **Limit the length of your slide presentations to 20 minutes.** If you show a different slide on average every 15 seconds, you will be able to show 80 slides in 20 minutes. This length of time is short enough that you won't put people to sleep, yet long enough to cover a substantial chunk of information. If your slide presentation is longer than 20 minutes, display a filler slide at the 20-minute marker so you can turn up the lights and answer questions before resuming with the next portion of the presentation. Breaking every 20 minutes keeps participants alert.

- **Make sure your slides depict diversity.** Even if your audience is homogeneous, it is important that those viewing your presentation see that you have taken the time to take slides that depict the rich diversity of the early childhood field. This applies to pictures of children as well as adults.

- **Have a backup plan.** As sure as winter comes to Iceland, there will be a day when you arrive for your workshop and there is no slide projector for your presentation. Make sure you have a backup plan. My colleague Eileen Eisenberg, who does a lot of training on learning environments, has converted many of her slides and color photographs to overhead transparencies. Her preference is to use the slides because the pictures are more crisp and clear, but she is prepared in the event that only an overhead projector is available for her presentation.

Videos

When selected carefully and used judiciously, videos can be a powerful visual aid in your workshops. You can show a video in its entirety to reinforce key concepts in your workshop or have participants view preselected segments that augment important points you make. The key to using videos effectively is to know how to integrate them into the design of your workshop so that they are an integral part of the learning experience. Peggy Sharp suggests these advantages of using videotapes in workshops:

✔ Video is attention getting and persuasive.
✔ Video is a quick way to provide a common experience.
✔ Video shows process and motion.
✔ Video provides participants with an opportunity to hear important concepts from the experts who developed them.
✔ Video can be shown in a partially lighted room.
✔ Video involves viewers emotionally and intellectually.
✔ Videos can be viewed repeatedly for review.
✔ Video cassettes are easy to use.
✔ Motion image sequences can be slowed down, allowing participants an opportunity to view a particular skill in slow motion for greater comprehension.

While videos can provide a welcome change of pace and help you achieve your workshop goals, there are some distinct disadvantages to this medium. Peggy Sharp mentions the following:

✔ Video is only suitable for small groups unless several monitors or projectors are used.
✔ Renting the necessary projection equipment for video can be expensive.
✔ Video is inflexible in that not all of what is on the tape will relate to your workshop.
✔ Participants may be lulled into viewing passively, in much the same way that people watch television at home.
✔ The production quality of many training videos is not good.

Guidelines for using videos

When considering whether or not to use a video in your workshop, ask yourself these questions:

✔ Does the video support my overall workshop goals?
✔ Does the video communicate concepts and ideas better than any other medium?
✔ Are the images, sound, music, and other aspects of the production of high quality?
✔ Is the video sufficiently compelling to sustain participants' interest?
✔ Does the video portray diversity?

Never show a video without previewing it first. Become thoroughly familiar with both the content and the timing of the video. Familiarity with the content gives you the background you need to develop meaningful viewing guidelines for the participants. Familiarity with the timing of the video allows you to incorporate its use in your workshop in the most efficient and effective way. For example, you may want to schedule its viewing right before lunch to facilitate discussion about the video during lunch.

When you introduce the video, tell participants what they will see. Let them know if you want them to take notes during the viewing or just watch attentively. Provide guidelines on what to look for during the video. You may even assign roles. One group of participants could look for practical examples that could be applied at the workplace. Another group might look for ideas that support or challenge their current beliefs. Still another group could look for unanswered questions that surface during viewing. In your introduction to the video, also let participants know what they will do immediately after the video. Will there be a discussion about key concepts, will they have a short quiz on the contents, or will they have a chance to share their personal reactions?

Some training experts suggest you should not have more than 20 minutes of video presentation during any hour of your workshop. If the video is longer than 20 minutes, you should take a short break and return to it at a later point. While 20 minutes provides a good guideline for accommodating people's attention span, some videos may warrant a viewing without interruption even if they are longer.

A few other suggestions:

- ✔ Use a remote to stop and start the recording. That way you won't need to turn your back to participants while you operate the equipment.
- ✔ Play the videotape prior to beginning the workshop so you know how to operate the equipment.
- ✔ Dim the lights in the room about halfway — dark enough to facilitate easy viewing, but light enough for note taking and discouraging people from dozing off.
- ✔ Use the freeze-frame control to stop the machine when you want to call people's attention to a portion of the video or lead a short discussion about its content.

Creative adaptations

Consider creating your own video productions. Although they won't be very polished or professional looking from a technical standpoint, they can still serve as powerful teaching tools because they focus on the issues you deem most important. Short segments of children at play, teacher-child interactions, or different aspects of the learning environment can be woven into your workshop at appropriate points. Since the sound quality of your homemade production may leave something to be desired, you will probably want to turn it off and provide a narration.

If you are going to undertake your own recording, be sure to get a signed release for all teachers and children filmed. Appendix P is an example of a release form you can duplicate for this purpose.

Another creative adaptation in using videos is to put together your own collection of vignettes from different movies that illustrate important points of your training. For a workshop on interpersonal communication, for example, I've assembled about ten different short scenes from blockbuster movies that capture key aspects of effective and ineffective communication. Each scene is only three or four minutes in length, but juxtaposed with each other they make for entertaining viewing.

Flip Charts

Flip charts are an indispensable tool for workshop leaders. They can be used to reinforce what you say and help participants to structure their note taking. Flip charts can also be used to record participants' ideas during training. When used this way, they add to the collaborative spirit of the learning enterprise. As contributions are being recorded, people's experience and expertise is validated and the training environment takes on a collective sense of ownership.

In *Sharing Your Good Ideas*, Peggy Sharp highlights some additional advantages to using flip charts:

- ✔ Flip chart paper and easels are inexpensive.
- ✔ Flip charts can be adapted to a variety of situations.
- ✔ Flip charts can be made as participants speak, addressing the specific needs of a particular audience.
- ✔ Using a flip chart does not require special lighting.
- ✔ Flip charts are helpful organizers during a workshop because the pages are in sequential order.
- ✔ Flip charts aid in the retention of important information.

The biggest disadvantage of using flip charts is that they are suitable only if your group is relatively small, fewer than 40 people. Individuals sitting in the back of the room in a larger workshop will not be able to see them. Also, because writing on a flip chart requires that you turn your back to the audience, you lose eye contact with participants (and possibly control of the group) while you write. If not used properly, they can actually undermine the rapport you have established with the group.

Basic design tips for flip charts

No getting around it, you need neat handwriting to effectively use flip charts. If your penmanship looks like you write with your eyes closed, don't despair. There are ways to get around this handicap. You can prepare many of your flip chart pages before the workshop when you can take more time to concentrate on the appearance of your lettering (or coax a friend to do them for you). For those flip charts that need to be done on the spot, you can select a participant from the group who has good handwriting to help you out. Here are some suggestions for creating eye-appealing flip charts.

- **Use color deliberately.** Different colors evoke different emotions in people. Cool colors are calm and relaxing. They include blue, turquoise, purple, brown, dark green, and black. Use cool colors for the text on each page. Hot colors include fuchsia, orange, and red. Because hot colors grab attention, use them sparingly and for emphasis only. Hot colors can be used for key words, bullets, or special effects. Highlighters are soft pale colors. You can use yellow, light blue, light green, or light orange highlighter pens for filling in solid areas, shading, and other special effects.

- **Use watercolor markers.** Use watercolor markers instead of permanent marking pens. They won't bleed through to the next page or leave permanent stains on your clothes. My favorite markers are Sanford's Mr. Sketch pens. The come in twelve bold colors. When you use markers, write using the flat side of the marker to make letters bold.

- **Alternate colors.** Using a variety of colors on your flip chart pages makes them more eye-catching and easier to read from a distance. As a general rule, however, don't use more than four colors on any one page. Black, blue, purple, and green are good for text because they can be read easily from a distance. Select two colors for your text and alternate each bulleted point with a different color. Use a bold color for your title, and accent with a hot color like red, fuchsia, or orange.

- **Use capital letters for titles, lowercase for details.** Your flip charts will take on a professional look if you provide a title in capital letters at the top of the page. The standard rule for lettering is that it should be 1" tall for each 15 feet of distance for viewing. That means for a room that can accommodate a group of 30 people, your title should probably be about 3 to 4 inches tall and your text about 2 to 3 inches tall. If you use flip chart paper with 1 inch light blue grids, you'll find it is easier to make your lettering straight and even.

- **Be creative with your lettering.** Add variety to your flip charts by using overlapping letters, cursive, puffy letters, and shaded letters. With a little practice you can create some eye-catching flip charts that enliven your message.

AGENDA

BOOKLIST

STRESS

TEAMWORK

CHILDREN

● **Add bullets and borders for impact.** You can use stars, boxes, circles, diamonds, or just about any other symbol or geometric shape for bullets. For an added touch, use gold notary stickers or large foil stick-on stars for bullet points. Number items only if they relate specifically to a numerical sequence or hierarchy of ideas.

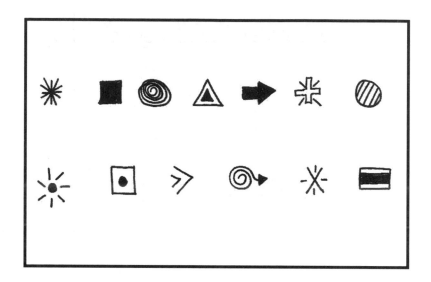

Adding a border helps set off your message. Use one of the colors you used for lettering to make your border, then add a thin line inside the border for accent. Use a hot color like red, orange, or fuchsia for this accent border

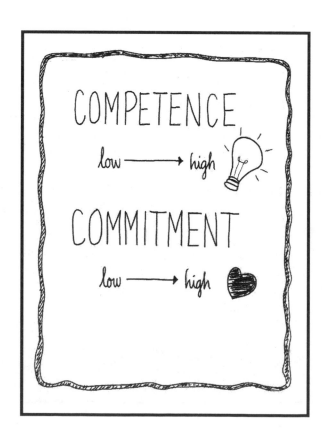

- **Avoid flip charts that are text heavy.** Use flip charts to capture key words and phrases that relate to the content you are talking about. Try to avoid writing out complete sentences, otherwise the paper will look too busy and it will be too difficult to read from a distance. Leave the bottom third of the page blank.

- **Use pointers to accent important information.** Cut out an arrow from large, color Post-it Notes to serve as a pointer. Stick your pointer on your flip chart whenever you want to draw attention to a specific item.

- **Use flag identifiers.** Post-it Tape Flags come in a variety of sizes and colors. You can attach these to the edge of a flip chart page to help you identify a specific chart you may want to turn to. This is particularly helpful if you will be referring back to a chart several times during your training. As a no-frills alternative, you can make a tab out of masking tape.

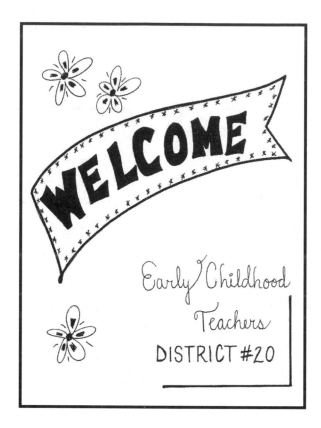

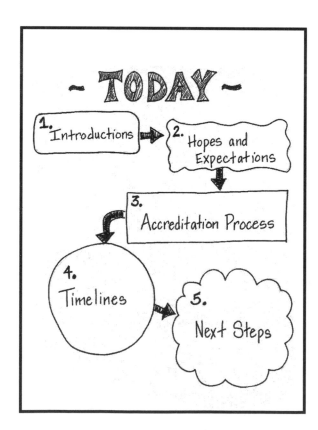

- **Add illustrations and graphics.** A cartoon, or pictograph, or a simple ideagram can add emphasis and call attention to your message. You don't need to be a talented illustrator. With practice you can master a dozen simple drawings to use repeatedly. If you want a more professional look to your illustrations, you can clip drawings from coloring books and trace the images onto the flip chart paper. If the drawing isn't large enough for your purposes, use an overhead projector to magnify the size of the object. Simply make a transparency of the cartoon or drawing on a photocopier, then project it onto the flip chart in the correct size and draw it with markers.

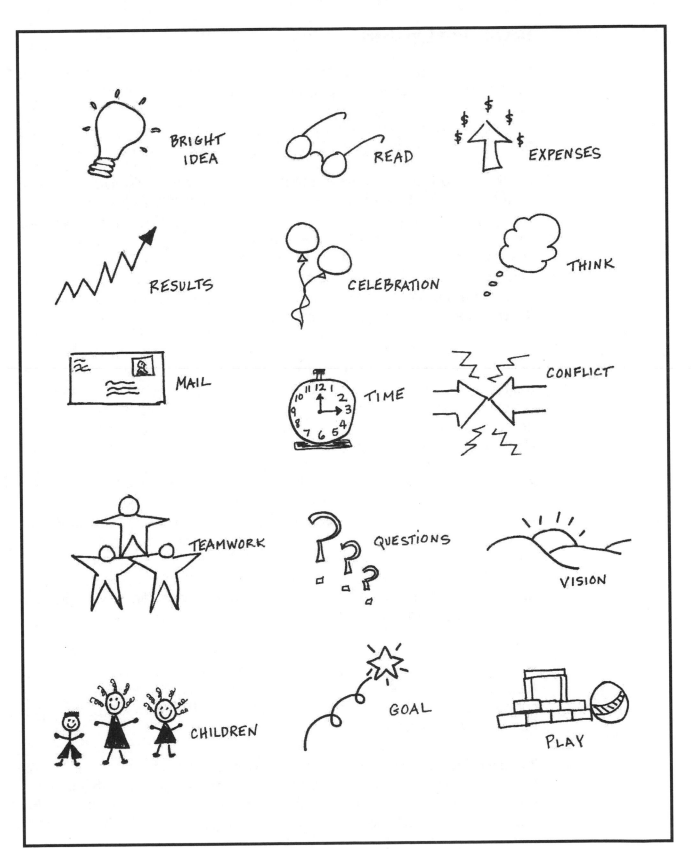

BRIGHT IDEA

READ

EXPENSES

RESULTS

CELEBRATION

THINK

MAIL

TIME

CONFLICT

TEAMWORK

QUESTIONS

VISION

CHILDREN

GOAL

PLAY

How to use flip charts

I've found it helpful to equip my training room with two flip charts. On one I put previously prepared material; the other I reserve for new information generated by the group. If you prepare some of your charts in advance, be sure to leave two or three blank sheets of paper between your prepared pages to keep them from being visible as you flip over a chart you have used.

In addition to the two easels in the front of the room, I usually post several pieces of flip chart paper on the walls. These might be labeled "Unfinished Business," "Needs Clarification," "Next Time," depending on the nature of the training. Sometimes I create a picture of a parking lot on a piece of flip chart paper that I post on the wall. I bring along a stack of Post-it Notes that have been cut in the shape of a car. When someone asks a question or an issue comes up that I want to put on hold until later, I ask the person to write the question on the Post-it Note car and park it in the parking lot.

When you use flip chart pages to record information from participants, write only the key words that reflect each contributor's ideas. Listen attentively to the comment, then turn to record. If you must talk while you are facing the flip chart, increase the volume of your voice. A better strategy is to ask one of the participants to serve as recorder. This frees you to facilitate the group, clarify ideas, and call on people.

When you are going to refer to something on your flip chart, stand to the side of the easel as you speak. Place yourself, your visual, and your audience in a triangular position. Then angle yourself to the side between your visual and your audience so you can see them both. This means your audience won't have to choose between you and your visual. Learn to direct the focus of your audience where you want it. You can even touch the information that you're talking about. Once you are finished referring to a page, flip it over and take a step or two toward the audience to recapture their attention.

If there are flip chart pages you want to refer back to or use as a reminder of information that has been discussed during the workshop, tear them off and tape them to the wall. Have several one-inch strips of masking tape already cut and posted on the side of the flip chart easel. This facilitates quick paper hanging during your session.

If you've invested a great deal of time preparing your flip charts, you'll want to save your work for future use. Stack each chart in order with a blank sheet between them. Use large paper clips or clamps to clip them together at the top. Store flat or roll and secure with a rubber band.

Computer-Assisted Presentations

With the advent of LCD projectors and presentation software like Microsoft PowerPoint and Lotus Freelance Graphics, preparing professional looking presentations is as easy as clicking a mouse. Years ago only high-price graphic artists had the skill to pull together slick multimedia presentations. Now every workshop trainer who has access to a computer and software can create powerful computer-assisted presentations that'll knock your socks off.

If you have basic computer skills, PowerPoint and Freelance Graphics can be powerful tools in your training arsenal. Presentation software can help you create a customized look for your presentation with slide masters, color palettes, and design templates. These programs also allow you to import clip art, photographs, and other pictures for added emphasis. You can give your presentation a high-tech look using AutoShape to add 3-D effects, embossing, and other special effects. The programs also allow you to make notes pages and handouts tied to your slides that participants can use as reference when your training is over.

Another advantage to computer-assisted presentations is that you can use hyperlinks to show additional resources (for example, links to forms, newsletters, brochures) that you have scanned and saved on your computer's hard drive. You can also link to other Web pages and provide a world of Internet resources for your participants.

While computer-assisted presentations can be great, they are definitely risky. Like any presentation that relies heavily on equipment, you need a well-rehearsed backup plan in case you encounter technical problems. Some trainers have resisted going the LCD route because they believe it makes their presentations appear too slick and interferes with the human dimension of establishing rapport and connecting with the audience.

Another disadvantage of computer-assisted presentations is that most hotels and conference facilities charge a hefty fee for rental of LCD projectors and laptop computers. You can avoid the expense if you bring your own equipment with you, but then you have the added inconvenience of lugging a projector and computer with you in addition to your handouts and other training supplies.

Equipment basics

To give a computer-assisted presentation, you need a computer and an active matrix LCD projector or RGB graphics projector. LCD stands for Liquid Crystal Display. An RGB graphics projector is not as portable as an LCD projector. However, it supports more standards and provides excellent projection in a very large room — about two or three times the light of the LCD projector.

If you are thinking about investing in your own LCD projector, here are a few suggestions to guide your purchase:

✔ Select a unit that is compatible with many different types of devices, including VGA, SVGA, XGA, and MAC.
✔ A good resolution is 800x600.
✔ Select a unit with a powerful enough lamp: 600-800 lumens is good; 1200 or above is excellent. The bulb is the most expensive part of the projector and, on average, lasts 1000 hours.
✔ Select a unit based on your need for portability — no more than 10 lbs. if you take your equipment on the road.

If you will be using a computer other than your own for your presentation, make sure it has the proper software (and correct version) installed on it. Be aware that the fonts you have used may not be installed in the computer you will be borrowing. This includes the specific type of bullet you've selected as well.

Always use AC power with your laptop computer and bring an extension cord and power strip to make sure you can plug in everything you need. It is preferable to use a mouse if you're using a laptop computer. You'll be able to manipulate it with more control than using the pointer on the computer. If you have incorporated sound into your presentation, make sure the projector comes equipped with an internal speaker or bring external speakers with you. Prior to your workshop, disable your screen saver and disable any system sounds that might interrupt your presentation.

Part of orchestrating a good presentation is making sure the room setup is conducive to using this type of audiovisual. Of particular importance is the screen and lighting. The ability to read your screen depends on character height and image contrast. Sit in the last row and make sure you can see and read all words projected on the screen without squinting. Set the lighting in your room dim enough to provide contrast to see the images on the screen yet bright enough to take notes.

Getting started

In her article *Anatomy of a Great Presentation*, Patricia Calderon offers some pointers on getting started. In PowerPoint, select File/New and pick a template from either the Presentation Designs or Presentations tab (which contains templates for specific topics). In Freelance Graphics select File/New Presentation and choose a content topic or design template. If you change your mind after developing your content, you can replace the template for all your slides by selecting Apply Design from PowerPoint's Common Tasks toolbar or by selecting Presentation/Choose A Different SmartMaster in Freelance Graphics. If you have a specific format you want to follow, both applications allow you to create custom templates.

If you want to use a graphic to emphasize a point, both PowerPoint and Freelance Graphics let you import a variety of image file formats — BMP, EPS, GIF, JPG, PCT, PCX, PNG, TIF, as well as clip art. Keep in mind that images will increase your presentation file size and slow down playback. Size your image to the exact height and width needed. Also make sure the resolution of the image is set to 72 dpi (dots per inch), and save it as an RGB image. If you use the same image more than once, copy and paste it from slide to slide; don't reimport it.

As you design your presentation slides, here are some pointers:

- **Avoid specialty fonts.** Unusual or fancy typefaces can be difficult to read. Use 16-point or larger type. Limit the number of fonts to no more than two typefaces throughout your presentation.

- **Select standard colors for your templates.** You'll generally get better results with the base palette in each application. Use the same background for all slides you are using in your presentation. Stay away from patterned or busy backgrounds. The goal is to give a consistent look to your slides.

- **Stick to one graphic style.** If you use clip art in one portion of your presentation, use clip art throughout. Use the same background image, color schemes, and bullet-point graphics in all your slides.

- **Use multimedia elements sparingly.** Special effects such as animation should be used in moderation. Special effects and transitions should serve as visual cues that tell your audience what to look at and in what order. They should follow a pattern to avoid visual chaos. If you use too many special effects and transitions, the participants in your workshop will focus on the packaging instead of the content. If you use a headline effect such as a wipe-right or fly-from-left, for example, it should always be the same. Bullet points should also build in the same way on each slide.

- **Vary your pacing.** Every mouse click or transition should not be spaced equally apart. Vary your pacing to give some auditory and visual variety to your audience.

- **Test your presentation on the equipment you will be using.** Both PowerPoint and Freelance Graphics let you embed stand-alone video, music, or sound effects that are triggered automatically or by a mouse action. But the actual execution of these effects can vary depending on your equipment. Be sure to test all effects on the equipment you'll be using to make sure everything goes as planned.

- **Don't let your medium overwhelm your message.** One of the biggest mistakes people make in creating computer-assisted presentations is using too many slides. They wear out their audience with visual overdose. Keep this in mind as you design your presentation.

There are several resources that can help you as you develop your skills in designing computer-assisted presentations. Chip Donohue provides step-by-step instructions on how to use Freelance Graphics in his book *Lotus SmartSuite: A Training Manual for Child Care Directors.* Microsoft publishes a monthly newsletter *Inside Microsoft PowerPoint* that contains tips and techniques for using PowerPoint. It can be ordered by calling 800-223-8720. Several of the Websites listed in the back of this book also include information about designing high impact computer-assisted presentations.

A high-tech, high-touch alternative

If you feel that a computer-assisted presentation may be a bit stiff and formal for your workshop, you can still harness the power of computer technology for preparing your workshop. Use PowerPoint or Freelance Graphics applications to make your handouts and transparencies. On the following page you'll find an example of a handout I made using PowerPoint. The images on the following page correspond to the transparencies used in the workshop. With other computer applications you can generate custom-designed crossword puzzles and games that include electronic clip art and graphics.

A Framework for Shared Decision Making

- Who are the stakeholders?
- What are the different types of decisions to be made?
- What are the possible levels of participation?
- What are the external constraints?

External Constraints

- time
- resources
- mandates
- staff stability

The person who insists upon seeing with perfect clearness before he decides,

never decides.

Henri Frederic Amiel

Props

Using props as a visual aid is a surefire way to grab attention. They can add interest and variety to a workshop and make your points more memorable. The key to using props, however, is that they must have a purpose. If a prop you use does not relate in some way to your workshop goals, it will be perceived as gratuitous entertainment.

Props can be simple or elaborate, homespun or purchased, ordinary or novel. The possibilities are limitless. After you've designed the content of your workshop, think of the specific subtopics you will be covering and the points you want to make. Then ask yourself if there is a way to incorporate a prop that would help dramatize or make your point.

Some personal examples

I love using props. Some of my props are serious, but most are light-hearted and fun and intended to interject some levity into the training environment. The key to using props, I have found, is to keep them hidden until you are ready to use them. Make sure the prop can be seen from all parts of the room. And if it is a prop you hold, make sure you talk to the group and not the prop. Here are a few examples of how I have incorporated props into my training.

✔ In a workshop on leadership, I bring in a box of different hats to dramatize the multifaceted nature of the director's job. As I put each hat on my head — firefighter, policeman, artist, plumber, nurse, captain, coach, accountant — I talk using metaphors about that aspect of the director's job.

✔ In a workshop on interpersonal communication, I always share the quote, "Before I can walk in another person's shoes, I must first remove my own," to emphasize the importance of understanding another person's perspective on an issue. Shortly after sharing the quote, I slip off my shoes and put on a large pair of men's shoes. I stand before the group and share a personal story of a time I had to figuratively remove my own shoes before I could understand a coworker with whom I had a difference of opinion.

✔ When training on how to conduct effective meetings, I like to underscore the importance of considering the opinions of people who are not present at the meeting. To do this I bring in a life-size cutout of a person that I've made out of butcher paper. I put a name like *Martha* on the cutout and sit the paper figure in a chair. During a mock staff meeting in which participants role play as part of the workshop, Martha is one of the characters. At different points during the dramatized staff meeting, the actors are encouraged to say, "I wonder what Martha might say about this issue if she were here?"

✔ In a workshop on conflict resolution, I distribute a large paper clip to each person. During the workshop, participants have an opportunity to talk about a situation that damaged their relationship with another person. I ask them to stretch out the paper clip as they talk about the situation. Then we talk about how to put the paper clip back in its original shape. The point, of course, is that it can never be put back precisely as it was before it was bent out of shape. Metaphorically we play through the significance of that point.

✔ At the beginning of a workshop on appreciating individual differences, I distribute a potato to each person. The potatoes are varied in size, shape, and texture. I include as many varieties as the local supermarket carries — sweet potatoes, redskins, russet, Yukon gold, ruby crescent, Idaho white, and others. I intentionally bring in a few that have been sitting in my pantry for several months and have grown some curious-looking sprouts. I then divide people into small groups and ask them to come up with all the ways that spuds differ. This assignment always elicits much laughter. After a period of time, we share the results of the group deliberations. I then ask the groups to discuss all the ways that people are like potatoes. This generates even more laughter as they come up with all kinds of silly and serious similarities. Finally, we circle back and relate their insights to the topic for the day.

✔ In a workshop on job satisfaction after a discussion about different job values, I distribute some play money to people and ask them to "purchase" those values that are most important to their sense of professional fulfillment. Participants have a chance to pay different amounts of money for the job values most important to them — autonomy, creativity, intellectual stimulation, recognition, security. This activity gets them thinking about the weight or importance of different aspects of their jobs.

✔ In leading a workshop for directors on organizational change, I usually begin by talking about health — the informal and formal ways a doctor diagnoses a person's health. To illustrate my point, I pull out a preschool doctor's kit and pretend to examine one of the participants. (I always ask their permission before the session begins.) I ask the person (usually a female) some informal questions: Does she work late hours? Does she have small children sneezing in her face? Does she lift heavy objects? These questions always rouse a chuckle from directors. Then I pretend to do some formal assessments (blood count, hold up an x-ray). After I render my doctorly opinion that she needs a paid sabbatical, I turn the attention of the group to a discussion about organizational health and the informal and formal ways they can assess it.

Standard props

There are some standard props I use in several workshops because there are similar types of situations that occur during training regardless of the topic. For example, I usually bring my magic wand with me when I conduct training. I keep it hidden in my prop box until someone in the group talks about an injustice they are experiencing as a result of some local, state, or federal mandate. At a moment when I want to turn griping into problem solving, I pull out my magic wand and hand it to the person. I then ask, "If you could change any one thing to make the situation better, what would it be?"

Another prop I use in a number of workshops is a giant Band-Aid (about 5 x 20 inches) that I purchased from a training supplies catalog. When someone in the group talks about a problem they are experiencing in their center, I ask them if it is a small boo-boo or a big boo-boo. They usually say it is a big boo-boo. At that moment I bring out the giant Band-Aid and talk about how they can cover up and ignore the problem or give it some air and try to solve the problem.

Children's books are excellent props to reinforce points in your workshop. You can read the book to the whole group, holding it up and turning the pages like you would in circle time for preschoolers, or you can convert the pictures in the book to transparencies and display them on an overhead projector. As an alternative, you can distribute books to small groups and have the participants read and discuss the relevance of the selection to the workshop topic. Here are just a few that I use in my leadership and management training:

Creating a vision
- ✔ *Harold and the Purple Crayon*, by Crocket Johnson
- ✔ *In the Attic*, by Hiawyn Oram
- ✔ *If I Were in Charge of the World and Other Worries*, by Judith Viorst
- ✔ *The Next Best Place*, by Warren Hanson
- ✔ *Under the Moon*, by Dyan Sheldon
- ✔ *Dear Mr. Blueberry*, by Simon James
- ✔ *The Salamander Room*, by Anne Mazer

Appreciating individual differences
  ✔ *A Bad Case of Stripes*, by David Shannon

Problem solving
  ✔ *The Boat*, by Monique Felix
  ✔ *Wilfrid Gordon McDonald Partridge*, by Mem Fox
  ✔ *Kind Bidgood's in the Bathtub*, Audrey Wood

Personal fulfillment
  ✔ *The Table Where Rich People Sit*, by Byrd Baylor

Perspective taking
  ✔ *Look-Alikes*, by Joan Steiner
  ✔ *Look-Alikes Jr.*, by Joan Steiner
  ✔ *Look! Look! Look!*, by Tana Hoban
  ✔ *Look Again!*, by Tana Hoban

Mentoring
  ✔ *The Other Way to Listen*, by Byrd Baylor

Sources for props

Your child's toy box, a preschool storage closet, or a resale shop are places you'll find wild and wonderful props to use in your training. Once you let your imagination take off, you'll search out new possibilities. Training supplies catalogues are also a great source for standard props. My favorite is

  ✔ The Trainer's Warehouse
    89 Washington Avenue
    Natick, MA 01760
    800-299-3770
    www.trainerswarehouse.com

Wrapping Things Up

Workshop leaders too often end their sessions in a frenzied state, looking at their watches and apologizing to participants for all the things they didn't get a chance to cover. They hurriedly distribute evaluation forms, ask if there are any final questions, and scurry people out the door while they pack up their markers and put on their coats.

Just as you started your workshop with an energizing opening, you need to end it with a closing that will leave a lasting impression on participants. Your closing is the equivalent of fireworks on the Fourth of July. It is the exclamation point to your presentation — that final touch that makes your workshop truly memorable.

The Importance of Closings

Closings should be a deliberate part of your workshop design, not something that just happens. The purpose of your closing is to:

- ✔ summarize key points covered during the workshop
- ✔ celebrate new knowledge and insights gained
- ✔ reinforce a sense of community
- ✔ motivate people to think about and practice what they have learned during the workshop

Your closing needs to be well orchestrated because you want to make sure you have enough time to accomplish these four goals yet still end your workshop on time. If you plan your closing well, you should be able to accomplish all you need to and still leave time for that standing ovation.

The guideline I use is to plan 10 minutes of closing activities for an hour-long presentation and 30 minutes for a half-day workshop. In full-day workshops you have a bit more flexibility. If you do activities throughout the day to process and recall information, your closing could be as short as 15 minutes. On the other hand, if you reserve your closing as the time to have participants process, recall, and plan next steps for applying the information, you will probably need a full 45 minutes for your closing.

Summarizing key points

Think of a way you can help people connect the dots of the information they have learned. Is there a way you can dramatize a unifying concept you covered? Is there a story you can tell that captures the essence of your message? Is there a poem or quote you can read that makes your point? Your culminating remarks need to capture attention as well as communicate the importance of your ideas. They need to be concise and have high impact. Let me share two examples:

✔ In the *Trainer's Guide to Circle of Influence*, I include a culminating activity that underscores the key concept that the sharing of power and influence can increase a director's capacity to implement a high-quality program. I distribute candles to several participants and dim the lights in the room. I light my candle and say, "If I light a candle, a soft glow permeates this room. Now imagine that the light from this candle symbolizes all the power and influence you have as a director of a center." I then light the candle of one of the participants and say, "If you use your candle to light the candle held by one of your teachers, thus sharing your power and influence, what happens to your candle? What happens to the glow in the room?" I light the remaining candles and say, "Now think about the glow of your single candle as your ability to effect change; your ability to implement a high-quality program. If you share your power and influence with everyone on your staff, just think of the collective glow that your combined candlepower can produce; your collective ability to achieve your dream of a high-quality program." This closing takes only 10 minutes to do, but the effect is dramatic.

✔ In another workshop on organizational change, I use a culminating activity that I learned from Silvana Clark, a trainer in Washington. This activity takes about 20 minutes, and I use it to underscore the important role directors play as change agents and that change can bring unexpected results. I don a chef's hat and apron and tell the participants I am going to whip up a recipe for change. In front of the group, I mix one cup of cold water and one cup of Elmer's School Glue into a glass bowl. I explain that these are ordinary elements of an early childhood program. I then mix the elements of change — one tablespoon of Borax in ½ cup very hot water. I stir the mixture until the Borax is thoroughly dissolved. Finally, I pour the "change elements" into the "routine elements." The mixture instantly transforms into a puttylike substance. It's fun to stretch, it snaps when pulled, it bounces, it squishes between one's fingers, and the whole is nothing like any of its parts. After this demonstration I restate my point that change can bring results that are not only unforeseen, but more fun than they might be imagined. As participants leave the workshop, I give them the recipe and a sandwich bag containing Borax. They love it.

Celebrating new knowledge and insights

At some point during the closing, you need to come full circle and reconnect with the initial goals and expectations you stated at the beginning of your workshop. You can do this in several ways. You can simply review the workshop goals that you posted on the wall at the beginning of your session or have individuals retrieve the personal workshop goals they wrote during your introductory remarks. Ask for volunteers to share one or two insights they gleaned from the training. Alternatively, you can conduct an activity like "10 Questions," "Swap Shop," or "Flypaper" (mentioned in Chapter 9) to reinforce what participants have learned during the workshop.

An informal approach to promoting self-appraisal and celebrating new knowledge is to ask participants the following two open-ended questions: Where do you think you are now? Where do you think you were when you started? You can then ask for volunteers to share their personal reflections of growth with the whole group.

In introducing any of these activities, it is important to stress that you are looking for personal relevance. The new knowledge and insights that people take home from the training need not be earth-shattering stuff, merely relevant and meaningful to them. Consider giving a certificate of attendance to participants to acknowledge their hard work. I've included an example in Appendix Q.

Reinforcing a sense of community

For multiday workshops where some participants have developed friendships while attending the workshop together, it is important to recognize the collegial spirit that has developed and reinforce the importance of staying connected. In your closing provide an opportunity for people to give brief testimonials acknowledging the significance of new friendships and how someone in the group has contributed to their learning. If you do this, be clear about your time limits (30 seconds or less). I once witnessed a situation where the testimonials went on for over an hour. Each person felt they needed to be more effusive and emotional in their tribute to a colleague than the person before them.

If all participants agree, compile and distribute a roster of everyone's name and contact information. If you are computer savvy, you can even set up a listserv for a period of time following the workshop to help people keep connected.

Here are two additional activities you might try to reinforce a sense of community.

- **Web of connections.** I got this idea from my colleague, Liz Tertell, who used it as the culminating activity for a three-day training. Ask everyone to stand. Then hand a ball of yarn to one person and asks her or him to hold the loose end. Then ask that person to say something about one other individual in the group and how he or she contributed to the training by providing information, resources, support, or humor. The person speaking then tosses the ball of yarn to another person while still holding on to their end. The process continues until every person has said something about one other person in the group, and the group is literally tied together in a web of connections.

- **Surprise connections.** Distribute a piece of plain white paper to each person and ask them to write their name, telephone number, and one thing they hope to accomplish in 60 days as a result of attending the workshop. Then give detailed directions on how to make a paper airplane. When everyone has accomplished the aeronautical feat, blow a whistle to signal that they can sail their airplane across the room. Participants pick up the airplanes that land near them and toss them again, keeping the airspace of the room filled with flying objects until your whistle signals them to stop. A minute is long enough for this air parade. At the end of this activity, ask everyone to pick up one airplane, making sure no one has his or her own. In 60 days this person should call their secret copilot and ask them how they are progressing in accomplishing the goal they had hoped to achieve as a result of attending the workshop.

Motivating people to apply what they have learned

The unfortunate reality of training is that despite good intentions, people rarely find time to revisit their workshop notes. Once they return to work, the day-to-day demands of their job clamor for their attention. If you will not be doing some systematic follow-up with the participants in your workshop, it is imperative that you provide some opportunity during your training or at the end of your training to help participants envision how they will apply the knowledge and information they have learned during your workshop.

Take a look again at the activities described in Chapter 9 in the section "Helping Participants Process and Recall Information." There are several activities in this section that are particularly good culminating activities to help your participants think about future applications. Depending on your time frame, consider the following: "A Contract with Myself," "Learning Partner Interview," "Turn and Tell," "Critical Incident," or "Action Plan." There is something about "going public" that helps people follow through with their good intentions.

Participant Evaluations

The old adage, "You can't please all the people all the time," is certainly true when it comes to training, but that does not diminish the importance of conducting an evaluation of your workshop. Evaluation is essential for two reasons: it communicates to participants that you care about what and how they learned, and it provides important information that will help you improve your workshop in the future.

Determining what questions to ask

While you can use a generic evaluation form, you will find you will get meatier feedback if you design one that is worded specifically for your topic. Unless you have some assistance in summarizing and analyzing the results, my recommendation is to keep the format simple and straightforward. A workshop evaluation form for a one-hour workshop should take no more than 5 minutes to complete, and for a half-day workshop, no more than 10 minutes to complete. For multiday training, the length of your evaluation will vary depending on your workshop goals and how you will use the information generated from the feedback.

In designing your workshop evaluation form, identify the criteria that reflect the specific information you want. Consider the following categories:

- ✔ facilities — location, room comfort
- ✔ food — quantity and quality
- ✔ organization of the workshop
- ✔ appropriateness of the content
- ✔ presenter's knowledge
- ✔ presenter's instructional style
- ✔ attention to personal needs
- ✔ usefulness of handouts
- ✔ usefulness of other visual aids

In addition, it is important to include a question or two that helps participants reflect on their own learning and behavior. Ask them to indicate the most important ideas or insights they gleaned from the session. You might also include a question about the effort they put forth and how they contributed to the group process. A final "any additional comments" question is useful because it elicits feedback that may not fit conveniently in one of the other categories. For example, a participant may want to compliment you on the way you handled a specific incident that occurred during the session or they may want you to send them a reference for a quote you used.

The format of your evaluation form can be serious and academic looking or it can be whimsical and humorous. You can structure your questions as open ended or as fixed response. Open-ended questions generally elicit richer qualitative data, but fixed-response or Likert-type scales are advantageous in that the data can be summarized into percentages or mean scores. An alternative format is to design an evaluation form that includes sentence completions.

Appendix R includes two examples of evaluation forms you can use or modify for your workshop. The first is a traditional evaluation form that includes both open-ended questions and rating scale questions. It was designed to evaluate the *Circle of Influence* workshop. The second is a generic form you can use that includes both sentence stems and rating scales.

If you don't want to use a formal evaluation form to elicit feedback, there are some informal and quick ways you can gather data from participants. Consider these two:

- **Pass the hat.** Distribute two small pieces of paper to participants and ask them on the first piece to write a number from 1 to 10 indicating their overall assessment of the workshop using the scale 1 = a waste of time to 10 = an energizing learning experience. On the second piece of paper ask them to write the most important thing they learned from the workshop. Pass a hat and ask people to drop their folded pieces of paper into the hat.

- **Post-it.** Tack three pieces of flip chart paper on the wall and distribute three Post-it Notes to each participant. On the three pieces of flip chart paper, write three questions or categories about which you'd like the group to provide feedback — the content of training, workshop logistics (timing, food, comfort), your presentation style. As they depart for the day, they can post their comments on the appropriate sheets of paper on the wall.

Distributing and collecting evaluation forms

Timing is an important issue when thinking about how to best conduct a workshop evaluation. The thing you want to avoid is having an upbeat closing that builds to a rousing crescendo and a round of applause, then spoil the effect by asking people to pull out their pens to fill out a form. It is anti-climactic and can ruin an otherwise perfect workshop. When people get an evaluation form distributed to them at the end of a workshop, when they are anxious to head home, they are less likely to take the time to give thoughtful feedback.

An alternative strategy is to distribute the evaluation form at the beginning of your workshop when you talk about goals and expectations for the day. Review the questions quickly at that time and let participants then know that you will be collecting the forms at the end of the day. Encourage people to take the time to complete the evaluation during their last break of the workshop. You will get higher quality responses when you give people more time to think about and complete the questions.

Anonymity and confidentiality

The issue of anonymity and confidentiality is also important to consider when deciding how to evaluate your workshop. Participants need be told who will read their evaluations and how the information will be used. There is a subtle but important difference between anonymity and confidentiality. Anonymity means that the person completing the form remains anonymous. You can ensure anonymity by having individuals put their evaluation forms in an envelope and asking them not to include their name on the form. Confidentiality means that the information shared on the form will be held in confidence and not shared with others.

In some instances you will want participants to put their names on their evaluation forms. For example, if your session is one of several you will be doing with the group and you want to tailor your training to the needs of individuals in the group, knowing what feedback came from which individuals is helpful. The downside of this approach is that people are generally more candid with their feedback when they are anonymous. An alternative is to put a place for the person's name on the evaluation form, but indicate that writing in their name is optional.

Taking Stock One More Time

Your moment of reckoning is upon you. You quickly thumb through the completed evaluation forms to sense if there are more tens than ones. You breathe a sigh of relieve. *They liked you!* Then you give a more careful reading to the open-ended comments, mentally highlighting those that you'll want to read again someday as a picker-upper when you're feeling down. While you gloat over the fact that the overall impression was very positive, you find yourself perseverating on those few comments that zeroed right in on your foibles. Ouch, those hurt!

So how do you put it all in perspective, knowing that you can't please all the people all the time? There will always be individuals who take exception to something you say or how you said it. And if they don't take exception to something you say, they'll take exception to something you didn't say but should have said. The reality is that not all your participants are going to hang on to your every word, be enthusiastic about every activity, and shower you with compliments at the end of your session.

The key is to look for patterns and not concentrate on specific comments that individuals make on their evaluation forms. It is in the patterns that you will get an accurate sense of how you did as a workshop leader. If only one or two people are annoyed with a particular strategy you used, the layout of your handouts, or the volume of your voice, take these comments seriously, but don't reengineer yourself or trash your workshop design to accommodate their grievances. On the other hand, if several people mention that your handouts are sloppy, your pace is too slow, or your visuals confusing, take these comments seriously and consider how you can improve.

Although feedback from participants is important, your self-evaluation is just as important. If you take time to critically assess how you did, you will glean useful information that will help you polish the tools in your presentation toolbox. Be honest with yourself as you answer the following questions:

Opening
- ✔ Did you start on time?
- ✔ Did your opening provoke interest and excitement about the topic?
- ✔ Did you review your goals and check the group's expectations?
- ✔ Did you preview the content of the workshop?

Body
- ✔ What instructional strategies worked exceptionally well?
- ✔ What instructional strategies need some fine-tuning?
- ✔ What portion of the time did you "teach and tell," and what portion did you allow people to discover personal meaning for themselves?
- ✔ Did your instructional strategies accommodate different learning styles?
- ✔ Did you use a variety of grouping strategies to get participants to build collegial interdependence?
- ✔ Did you present your content in an orderly, sequential fashion?
- ✔ Were your handouts organized and easy to follow?
- ✔ Were your visuals clear and understandable?
- ✔ Did you present the right amount of information?
- ✔ Did you allow enough time for activities and debriefing?

Appearance and delivery
- ✔ Did you look poised and confident?
- ✔ Were you well groomed?
- ✔ Did your voice project well?
- ✔ Were your movements purposeful?
- ✔ Were you warm and friendly?
- ✔ Were you able to achieve rapport?
- ✔ Did you exude enthusiasm about your topic?
- ✔ Were your notes organized and manageable?

Closing
- ✔ Did you close on a high note?
- ✔ Did you summarize key concepts?
- ✔ Did you thank people for attending?
- ✔ Did you validate the group's hard work?
- ✔ Did you reinforce personal connections?
- ✔ Did you end on time?

A Final Thought

We began this journey by talking about the developmental stages that characterize workshop leaders. If you are a novice presenter just venturing into the exciting yet intimidating world of workshop presentation, I hope the principles and practices outlined here have provided a blueprint to help you design and deliver a workshop that will boost your confidence and make you eager to do more. If you are a veteran presenter with more than a few notches on your belt, I hope the tips and techniques you read in these pages will help you hone your skills and make your presentations even more dynamic and memorable.

Regardless of your level of expertise in presenting, in the pursuit of excellence your own best resource is your commitment to lifelong learning and your willingness to take risks and experiment with new approaches that expand your repertoire. Continue to reflect on practice, taking mental notes on ways you can refine your skills. Observe other good trainers, adapting what fits your style. And continue to learn more about adult learning theory and group dynamics.

The road to becoming an accomplished workshop leader is an exciting journey of self-discovery. It is an empowering process that can lead to greater feelings of personal and professional fulfillment. Your payoff is the immense satisfaction you will feel knowing you have supported learning connections that in big and small ways transform the adults with whom you work and ultimately benefit the children in their care.

For Further Reading

Anton, T. (1997). *Wake 'em up!* Landover Hills, MD: Anchor.

Armstrong, D. (1992). *Managing by storying around: A new method of leadership.* New York: Doubleday.

Armstrong, T. (1994). *Multiple intelligences in the classroom.* Alexandria, VA: Association for Supervision and Curriculum Development.

Backer, L., & Deck, M. (1996). *The presenter's EZ graphics kit — A guide for the artistically challenged.* St. Louis: Mosby.

Barlow, C. A., Blythe, J., & Edmonds, M. (1999). *A handbook of interactive exercises for groups.* Boston: Allyn & Bacon.

Baron, D. (1999). *Moses on management.* New York: Pocket Books.

Bendaly, L. (1996). *Games teams play.* Toronto: McGraw-Hill Ryerson.

Bianchi, S., Butler, J., & Richey, D. (1990). *Warmups for meeting leaders.* San Diego, CA: University Associates.

Bloom, P. J. (2000). *Circle of influence.* Lake Forest, IL: New Horizons

Bloom, P. J. (2000). *Trainer's guide for circle of influence.* Lake Forest, IL: New Horizons.

Bloom, P. J. (2000). Images from the field: How directors view their organizations, their roles, and their jobs. In M. L. Culkin (Ed.), *Managing quality in young children's programs: The leader's role* (pp. 59-77). New York: Teachers College Press.

Bloom, P. J., Sheerer, M., & Britz, J. (1991). *Blueprint for action: Achieving center-based change through staff development.* Lake Forest, IL: New Horizons.

Brandt, R. C. (1986). *Flip charts: How to draw them and how to use them.* San Diego: University Associates.

Bredekamp, S., & Copple, C. (Eds.). (1997). *Developmentally appropriate practice in early childhood programs.* Rev. ed. Washington, DC: National Association for the Education of Young Children.

Brooks, J. G., & Brooks, M. G. (1993). *In search of understanding: The case for constructivist classrooms.* Alexandria, VA: Association for Supervision and Curriculum Development.

Brookfield, S. (1986). *Understanding and facilitating adult learning.* San Francisco: Jossey-Bass.

Caine, R., & Caine, G. (1997). *Education on the edge of possibility.* Alexandria, VA: Association for Supervision and Curriculum Development.

Calderon, P. (1998, June). Anatomy of a great presentation. *Windows Magazine*, 9(6), 200-13.

Campbell, D. (1997). *The Mozart effect.* New York: Avon.

Carter, M., & Curtis, D. (1998). *The visionary director: A handbook for dreaming, organizing, and improvising in your center.* St. Paul, MN: Redleaf.

Carter, M., & Curtis, D. (1994). *Training teachers.* St. Paul, MN: Redleaf.

Champion, R. (1999, Spring). Job aids boil it down. *Journal of Staff Development*, 63-65.

Clarke, J. I. (1984). *Who, me lead a group?* Seattle: Parenting Press.

Cross, K. P. (1981). *Adults as learners.* San Francisco: Jossey-Bass.

Diamondstone, J. (1980). *Designing, leading, and evaluating workshops for teachers and parents.* Ypsilanti, MI: High/Scope Educational Research Foundation.

Donohue, C. (2000). *Lotus SmartSuite: A training manual for child care directors.* Boston: WFD.

Dresser, N. (1996). *Multicultural manners: New rules for etiquette for a changing society.* New York: John Wiley.

Edelman, M. W. (1999). *Lanterns: A memoir of mentors.* Boston: Beacon.

Eitington, J. (1989). *The winning trainer.* Houston, TX: Gulf.

Fenchuk, G. W. (1998). *Timeless wisdom.* Midlothian, VA: Cake Eaters.

Gardner, H. (1999). *Intelligence reframed.* New York: Basic.

Garmston, R. (1997). *The presenter's fieldbook: A practical guide.* Norwood, MA: Christopher-Gordon.

Garmston, R. J., & Wellman, B. (1992). *How to make presentations that teach and transform.* Alexandria, VA: Association for Supervision and Curriculum Development.

Gregorc, A. (1982). *An adult's guide to style.* Maynard, MA: Gabriel Systems.

Grinder, M. (1991). *Righting the educational conveyer belt.* Portland, OR: Metamorphous.

Hackett, D., & Martin, C. (1993). *Facilitation skills for team leaders.* Menlo Park, CA: Crisp.

Hannaford, C. (1995). *Smart moves: Why learning is not all in your head.* Arlington, VA: Great Ocean.

Hart, L., (1991). *Training methods that work: A handbook for trainers.* Palo Alto, CA: Crisp.

Herman, B. (2000). Pathways to learning: An autobiographical inquiry into lessons from the middle. Doctoral dissertation, University of Illinois at Chicago.

Herman, B. (1999). *Teach me — reach me!* Deerfield, IL: Pathways to Learning.

Hunt, D. E. (1987). *Beginning with ourselves.* Cambridge, MA: Brookline Books.

Jackson, P. (1995). *Sacred hoops: Spiritual lessons of a hardwood warrior.* New York: Hyperion.

Jolles, R. (1993). *How to run seminars and workshops.* New York: John Wiley.

Jones, E. (1986). *Teaching adults. An active learning approach.* Washington, DC: National Association for the Education of Young Children.

Jones, E. (1993). *Growing teachers: Partnerships in staff development.* Washington, DC: National Association for the Education of Young Children.

Kalish, K. (1996, November). *How to give a terrific presentation.* New York: AMACOM, American Management Association.

Kearny, L. (1996). *Graphics for presenters: Getting your ideas across.* Palo Alto, CA: Crisp.

Kegan, R. (1994). *In over our heads: The mental demands of modern life.* Cambridge, MA: Harvard University Press.

Killion, J. P. (1999, Summer). Knowing when and how much to steer the ship. *Journal of Staff Development,* 20(1), 59-60.

Killion, J. P. (1988, Summer). Parallels between adult development and trainer development. *Journal of Staff Development* 9(3), 6-10.

Killion, J. P., & Simmons, L. (1992, Summer). The Zen of facilitation. *Journal of Staff Development,* 13(3), 2-5.

Knowles, M. S. (1980). *The modern practice of adult education: From pedagogy to andragogy.* Chicago: Follett.

Kolb, D. A. (1984). *Experiential learning.* Englewood Cliffs, NJ: Prentice-Hall.

Kopp, R. R. (1995). *Metaphor therapy.* New York: Bunner/Maxel.

Lipton, L., & Wellman, B. (1998). *Pathways to understanding: Patterns and practices in the learning-focused classroom.* Guilford, VT: Pathways.

McAfee, O. (1985, September). Getting to know you. *Child Care Information Exchange,* 13-15.

McCarthy, B. (1996). *About learning.* Barrington, IL: Excel.

McDonald, I. (1997). *Presentation skills profile.* King of Prussia, PA: Organization Design and Development.

Mandel, S. (1993). *Effective presentation skills: A practical guide for better speaking.* Palo Alto, CA: Crisp.

Martin, C., & Hackett, D. (1993). *Facilitation skills for team leaders.* Palo Alto, CA: Crisp.

Maxwell, J. C. (1998). *The 21 irrefutable laws of leadership.* Nashville: Thomas Nelson.

Merriam, S. B. (Ed.). (1989). *Being responsive to adult learners.* Glenview, IL: Scott Foresman.

Neugebauer, R. (1984, August). Making presentations: Avoiding the five deadly sins. *Child Care Information Exchange*, 2-12.

Newstrom, J., & Scannell E. (1996). *The big book of business games*. New York: McGraw-Hill.

Newstrom, J., & Scannell E. (1998). *The big book of presentation games*. New York: McGraw-Hill.

Ornstein, R. (1997). *The right mind: Making sense of the hemispheres*. San Diego, CA: Harcourt Brace.

Petit, A. (1994). *Secrets to enliven learning*. San Diego: Pfeiffer.

Pike, R. (1994). *Creative training techniques handbook*. Minneapolis, MN: Lakewood.

Poitier, S. (2000). *The measure of a man: A spiritual memoir*. San Francisco: HarperCollins.

Raines, C., & Williamson, L. (1995). *Using visual aids*. Palo Alto, CA: Crisp Publications.

Rand, M. K. (2000). *Giving it some thought. Cases for early childhood practice*. Washington, DC: National Association for the Education of Young Children.

Razran, G. (1938). Conditioning away social bias by the luncheon technique. *Psychological Bulletin*, 35, 693.

Scannell E., & Newstrom, J. (1991). *Games trainers play: Experiential learning exercises*. New York: McGraw-Hill.

Scannell E, & Newstrom, J. (1991). *More games trainers play: Experiential learning exercises*. New York: McGraw-Hill.

Sharp, P. (1993). *Sharing your good ideas: A workshop facilitator's handbook*. Portsmouth, NH: Heinemann.

Silberman, M. (1999). *101 ways to make meetings active*. San Francisco: Jossey-Bass/Pfeiffer.

Solem, L., & Pike, B. (1997). *Fifty creative training closures*. San Francisco: Jossey-Bass/Pfeiffer.

Sousa, D. (1995). *How the brain works.* Reston, VA: National Association of Secondary School Principals.

Steinbach, B. (1993). *The adult learner: Strategies for success.* Menlo Park, CA: Crisp.

Tobias, C. (1994). The way they learn. Colorado Springs, CO: Focus on the Family Publishing.

Van Daele, C. (1995). *Fifty one-minute tips for trainers.* Palo Alto, CA: Crisp.

Vella, J. (1994). *Learning to listen, learning to teach: The power of dialogue in educating adults.* San Francisco, Jossey-Bass.

Weinstein, M., & Goodman, J. (1980). *Playfair.* San Luis Obispo, CA: Impact.

Williamson, B. (1993). *Playful activities.* Duluth, MN: Whole Person Associates.

Wohlmuth, E. (1983). *The overnight guide to public speaking.* Philadelphia: Running Press.

Wurtman, J. (1986). *Managing your mind and mood through food.* New York: Harper & Row.

Internet Resources

Inspirational Quotes, Bits of Trivia, and Humorous One-Liners

- www.corsinet.com/braincandy
- www.greenleafenterprises.com/quotes.asp
- www.geocities.com/Athens/7186
- www.famous-quotations.com
- www.aphorismsgalore.com
- www.inspirationpeak.com
- www.llsten.org/pages/quotes
- www.oneliners-and-proverbs.com
- www.cyber-nation.com/victory/quotations
- www.motivateus.com
- www.justriddlesandmore.com
- www.mcn.net/~jimloy
- www.FunnyScott.com
- www.startpage.com
- www.starlingtech.com/quotes
- www.newsjoke.com
- www.swcbc.com/humor]
- www.cc.columbia.edu/acis/bartleby/bartlett
- www.jokeEmail.com

General Advice on Delivering Effective Presentations

- www.presentersuniversity.com

- www.winmag.com

- www.howto4u.com

- www.nsdc.org

- www.antion.com

- www.presentations.com

- www.startpage.com

- www.cooltext.com

- www.trainerswarehouse.com

- www.squarewheels.com

- www.thiagi.com

Appendices

Workshop Planning Form

Proposed workshop title _____

Date of workshop _____ Start time _____ End time _____

Contact person _____ Home phone _____

Organization _____ Phone _____

Address _____ Fax _____

City _____ State _____ ZIP _____

Total number of participants attending _____ Voluntary _____ Mandatory _____

Participants with special needs (physical disabilities, sight- or hearing-impaired):

Yes _____ No _____

Information about participants (background, problems, challenges, issues):

_____

_____

Needs assessments done: _____

Information about the organization (history, major events, problems, challenges):

_____

_____

Sensitive issues that should be avoided: _____

Workshop objectives: _____

Key concepts to cover: _____

_____

_____

_____

Possible stories, examples, visuals to emphasize key concepts: _____

_____

_____

_____

Travel arrangements_____

Airline _____ Phone _____

Outbound: Date _____ depart at_____ arrive at_____

Return trip: Date _____ depart at_____ arrive at_____

Connection from airport to hotel: Taxi _____ Rental care _____ Pick up_____

Hotel _____ Phone _____

Address _____ Reservation number _____

Location of workshop site _____ Phone _____

Room number _____Room setup_____

Publicity _____

Miscellaneous details: _____

_____

_____

_____

_____

_____

_____

_____

_____

Workshop Design Matrix

Time	Topic	Description	Method	Visual Aids

Getting to Know You

_____ I drive a minivan.

_____ I can do a cartwheel.

_____ I own a snow blower.

_____ I speak Hebrew.

_____ I have a tattoo.

_____ I play a musical instrument.

_____ I've been to Istanbul.

_____ I am allergic to bee stings.

_____ I am a Libra.

_____ I can tell the difference between a petunia and a pansy.

_____ I sleep on a waterbed.

_____ I drive a car that is more than 20 years old.

_____ I own a Dalmatian.

_____ I know how to change the oil filter on my car.

_____ I sing in the shower.

_____ I like ketchup with my scrambled eggs.

_____ I know all the words to our national anthem.

_____ I'm afraid of spiders.

_____ I've been up in a hot air balloon.

_____ I've run a marathon.

_____ I've been to a Bulls game.

_____ I know the names of the seven dwarfs.

Personal Traits

Adventurous	**Affectionate**	**Assertive**
Bright	**Bubbly**	**Calm**
Capable	**Carefree**	**Cheerful**
Compassionate	**Contemplative**	**Confident**
Considerate	**Creative**	**Down-to-earth**
Eager	**Easygoing**	**Energetic**
Experimental	**Expressive**	**Exuberant**
Fanciful	**Fearless**	**Flexible**

Forthright	Fragile	Fresh
Friendly	Funny	Generous
Graceful	Gregarious	Happy
Humorous	Helpful	Imaginative
Impatient	Impulsive	Ingenious
Innocent	Inquisitive	Intense
Joyful	Lively	Loving
Open	Optimistic	Organized
Patient	Perceptive	Persistent

Philosophical	Playful	Precise
Rambunctious	Reflective	Reserved
Resilient	Resourceful	Risk taker
Serious	Sensitive	Sharing
Shy	Silly	Sloppy
Soft-spoken	Spontaneous	Surprising
Talkative	Tenacious	Tireless
Trustworthy	Witty	Zestful

Name that Acronym

NAEYC	
ACEI	
CDF	
CCW	
CDA	
CCR&R	
NHSA	
NSACCA	
NBCDI	
NAFCC	
CECL	
ADA	
ADD	
FRCA	
ERIC/EECE	
WIC	
NIOST	
GAO	
NCCP	
CWLA	
ASCD	
CCAC	
NSDC	
TQM	
IDEA	
CACFP	
IEP	

Name that Acronym
Answers

NAEYC	National Association for the Education of Young Children
ACEI	Association for Childhood Education International
CDF	Children's Defense Fund
CCW	Center for the Child Care Workforce
CDA	Child Development Associate
CCR&R	Child Care Resource and Referral
NHSA	National Head Start Association
NSACCA	National School Age Child Care Alliance
NBCDI	National Black Child Development Institute
NAFCC	National Association for Family Child Care
CECL	The Center for Early Childhood Leadership
ADA	Americans with Disabilities Act
ADD	Attention Deficit Disorder
FRCA	Family Resource Coalition of America
ERIC/EECE	Educational Resources Information Center/Elementary and Early Childhood Education
WIC	Special Supplemental Food Program for Women, Infants, and Children
NIOST	National Institute for Out-of-School Time
GAO	U.S. Government Accounting Office
NCCP	National Center for Children in Poverty
CWLA	Child Welfare League of America
ASCD	Association for Supervision and Curriculum Development
CCAC	Child Care Action Campaign
NSDC	National Staff Development Council
TQM	Total Quality Management
IDEA	Individuals with Disabilities Education Act
CACFP	Child and Adult Care Food Program
IEP	Individualized Educational Plan

Things You Didn't Know You Didn't Know

1. A giraffe's tongue is how long?

2. Where does pound cake get its name?

3. How many divorces occur in the U.S. each day?

4. How many pounds of potatoes does it take to make one pound of potato chips?

5. How far does the average office chair on wheels travel a year?

6. How many days does it take for a snail to go one mile?

7. What size shoe did Robert E. Lee wear?

8. Where did kilts originate?

9. How many noses does an ant have?

10. How many credit cards does the average American carry?

11. What was J.C. Penney's middle name?

12. How much does an elephant's heart weigh?

13. How many telephone calls does the average person make in a year?

14. Who was our nation's only bachelor president?

15. What was Smokey the Bear's original name?

16. How many calories does a laugh burn?

17. How many different ways can you make change for a dollar?

Things You Didn't Know You Didn't Know

Answers

1. A giraffe's tongue is 17 inches long.

2. Pound cake gets its name from the pound of butter used to make it.

3. 3,000 divorces occur in the U.S. each day.

4. It takes 4 pounds of potatoes to get 1 pound of chips.

5. The average office chair on wheels goes 8 miles a year.

6. It takes 115 days for a snail to go a mile.

7. Robert E. Lee wore size 4 1/2 shoes.

8. Kilts originated in France.

9. An ant has 5 noses.

10. The average American carries 4 credit cards.

11. J.C. Penney's middle name was Cash.

12. An elephant's heart weighs 45 pounds.

13. The average person makes 1,140 telephone calls per year.

14. James Buchanan was the only bachelor president.

15. Smokey the Bear's original name was Hot Foot Teddy.

16. A laugh burns up to 3 1/2 calories.

17. There are 293 ways to make change for a dollar.

Brainteasers

1. SAND

2. MAN / BOARD

3. STAND / I

4. R|E|A|D|I|N|G

5. WEAR / LONG

6. R O A D (vertical R, A, D on ROAD)

7. CYCLE CYCLE CYCLE

8. T O W N (vertical)

9. LE VEL

10. 0 / M.D. / Ph.D. / D.D.S.

11. KNEE / LIGHT

12. ii ii / O O

13. CHAIR

14. DICE DICE

15. T O U C H (vertical)

16. GROUND / FEET FEET FEET FEET FEET FEET

17. MIND / MATTER

18. HE'S | HIMSELF

19. ECNALG

20. DEATH | LIFE

21. CRAZY / YOU

22. RETTAB (vertical)

23. YOU JUST ME (JUST vertical)

24. OATH / UR

25. WORHT (vertical)

26. C with LOUSE / B (club)

Brainteasers
Answers

1. Sandbox

2. Man over board

3. I understand

4. Reading between the lines

5. Long underwear

6. Crossroads

7. Tricycle

8. Downtown

9. Split level

10. 3 degrees below zero

11. Neon light

12. Circles under your eyes

13. High chair

14. Pair of dice

15. Touch down

16. Six feet underground

17. Mind over matter

18. He's beside himself

19. Backward glance

20. Life after death

21. Crazy over you

22. Batter up

23. Just between you and me

24. You're under oath

25. Throw up

26. See-through blouse

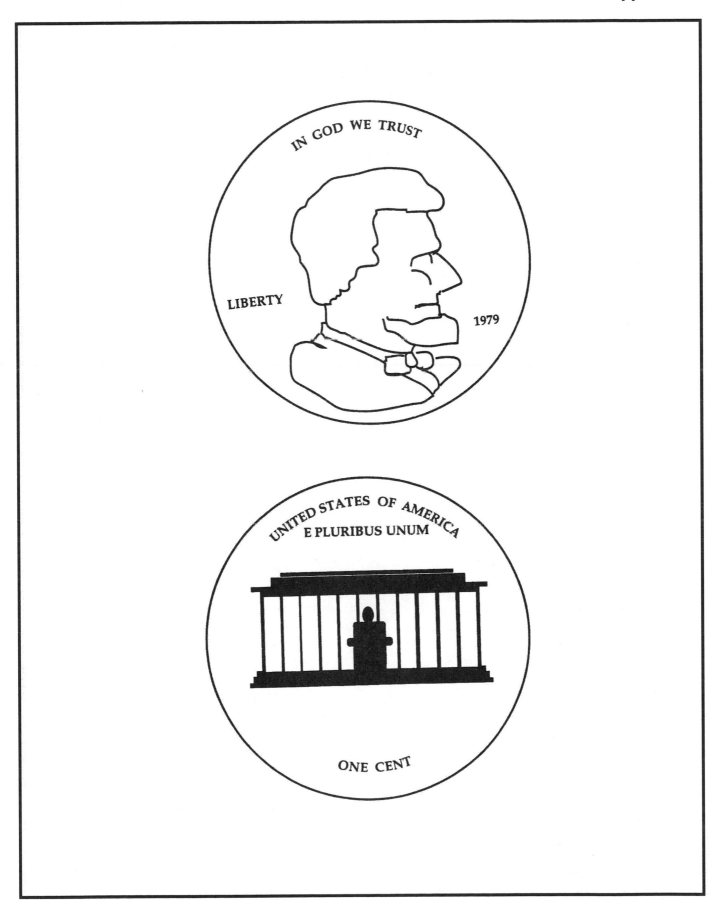

What's On a Penny?

Front side:

1. "In God We Trust"
2. "Liberty"
3. Date
4. Mint mark (under date, sometimes)
5. President Lincoln's portrait facing his left

Back side:

6. "United States of America"
7. "One Cent"
8. "E Pluribus Unum"
9. Lincoln Memorial (12 columns)
10. Lincoln statue in middle of columns

General:

11. It is copper colored.
12. The rim around the edge on both sides is raised
13. The front and back are inverted with respect to each other
14. The diameter is 3/4 inch.
15. The thickness is approximately 1/16 inch.
16. Its weight is approximately 1/6 ounce.
17. The external rim is smooth on the outside.

From Newstrom, J., & Scannell, E. (1996). <u>The big book of business games</u>. New York: McGraw-Hill, pp. 119-23. Reprinted with permission.

Making Connections

Bright Ideas

1. _____
2. _____
3. _____
4. _____
5. _____
6. _____
7. _____
8. _____
9. _____
10. _____
11. _____
12. _____
13. _____
14. _____
15. _____
16. _____
17. _____
18. _____
19. _____
20. _____

Reflections

Reflect on the personal relevance of this workshop for you. What new insights did you gain from this training experience? What previous beliefs or knowledge were validated? What new questions about your own role were prompted by your participation in this professional development experience?

_____

_____

_____

_____

_____

_____

_____

_____

_____

_____

_____

_____

_____

_____

_____

A Contract with Myself

I plan to use the information I have learned in this workshop to: _____

_____

_____

_____

I am going to share this information with: _____

_____

I plan to work on the following areas to increase my knowledge and skill: _____

_____

_____

_____

_____

_____

_____

_____

Signed _____

Date _____

Witness _____

Think Tank

?

YES!

NO!

Action Plan

Statement of the problem: _____

_____

_____

_____

My goal: _____

_____

Action steps	Resources needed	Target date
_____	_____	_____
_____	_____	_____
_____	_____	_____
_____	_____	_____
_____	_____	_____
_____	_____	_____
_____	_____	_____
_____	_____	_____
_____	_____	_____
_____	_____	_____
_____	_____	_____

Evaluation plan: _____

_____

_____

_____

Release Form

I authorize _____ to photograph or videotape my child, _____, and to use the photographs or video footage for educational purposes. I agree that I am to receive no compensation or ownership rights whatsoever.

Child's name: _____

Parent or guardian: _____

Date: _____

National-Louis University
1000 Capitol Drive
Wheeling, IL 60090-7201

The Center for
Early Childhood Leadership

Certificate of Completion

Awarded to

Directors' Technology Training

Awarded to

Rachel Meyer
February 21, 2000

Funding provided by the
Illinois Department of Human Services

Tim Walker, Instructor

Jill Bella, Classroom Assistant

CIRCLE OF INFLUENCE

Workshop Evaluation

Using a scale of 1-5 (1 = poor and 5 = excellent) evaluate the following:

_____ Length and format of the workshop

_____ Knowledge and instructional style of the trainer

_____ Overall usefulness of the material

_____ Training room comfort

_____ Attention to personal needs

The most important thing I learned in this workshop about shared decision making and participative management is . . .

I would like to learn more about . . .

One new idea I hope to try out when I return to my job is . . .

The following suggestions might help strengthen this workshop in the future:

Workshop Evaluation

In this workshop I learned that ...

As a result of this workshop, I plan to ...

_____
_____
_____
_____
_____
_____
_____
_____
_____
_____
_____
_____

The best part of the workshop was ...

For next time, think about ...

Overall, I would rate the workshop:

 0 – 1 – 2 – 3 – 4 – 5 – 6 – 7 – 8 – 9 – 10
poor   excellent

My participation level during this workshop was:

0 – 1 – 2 – 3 – 4 – 5 – 6 – 7 – 8 – 9 – 10
passive   very involved

Anything else you'd like to tell us:

Index

Available from New Horizons

Other Books by Paula Jorde Bloom

- *Circle of Influence: Implementing Shared Decision Making and Participative Management* $14.95

- *Trainer's Guide for Circle of Influence* $69.95

- *Avoiding Burnout: Strategies for Managing Time, Space, and People in Early Childhood Education* $14.95

- *Blueprint for Action: Achieving Center-Based Change Through Staff Development* $28.95

- *Blueprint for Action Assessment Tools Packet* $11.95

- *A Great Place to Work: Improving Conditions for Staff in Young Children's Programs* $6.00

To place your order or receive additional information
on quality discounts, contact:

NEW HORIZONS

P.O. Box 863
Lake Forest, IL 60045-0863
Telephone: (847) 295-8131, Fax (847) 295-2968